2nd Edition
ROI BASICS

Patricia Pulliam Phillips and Jack J. Phillips

atd PRESS

ROI INSTITUTE®

© 2019 ASTD DBA the Association for Talent Development (ATD)
All rights reserved. Printed in the United States of America.

22 21 20 19   1 2 3 4 5

No part of this publication may be reproduced, distributed, or transmitted in any form or by any means, including photocopying, recording, information storage and retrieval systems, or other electronic or mechanical methods, without the prior written permission of the publisher, except in the case of brief quotations embodied in critical reviews and certain other noncommercial uses permitted by copyright law. For permission requests, please go to www.copyright.com, or contact Copyright Clearance Center (CCC), 222 Rosewood Drive, Danvers, MA 01923 (telephone: 978.750.8400; fax: 978.646.8600).

ATD Press is an internationally renowned source of insightful and practical information on talent development, training, and professional development.

ATD Press
1640 King Street
Alexandria, VA 22314 USA

Ordering information: Books published by ATD Press can be purchased by visiting ATD's website at www.td.org/books or by calling 800.628.2783 or 703.683.8100.

Library of Congress Control Number: 2019948856

ISBN-10: 1-950496-37-6
ISBN-13: 978-1-950496-37-2
e-ISBN: 978-1-950496-38-9

ATD Press Editorial Staff
Director: Sarah Halgas
Manager: Melissa Jones
Community of Practice Manager, Senior Leaders & Executives: Ann Parker
Developmental Editor: Jack Harlow
Text and Cover Design: Shirley E.M. Raybuck

Printed by P.A. Hutchison Company, Mayfield, PA

Contents

About the Basics Series v
Preface vii

1. The Basics 1
    Defining ROI 2
    ROI and the Levels of Evaluation 5
    The Evaluation Puzzle 10
    The ROI Process Model 13
    Putting ROI to Use 17
    Getting It Done 21

2. Plan Your Work 25
    Aligning Programs With the Business 26
    The Alignment Model in Action 31
    Defining Program Objectives 33
    Developing the Evaluation Plan 39
    Getting It Done 52

3. Collect Data 55
    Selecting the Method 56
    Defining the Source 78
    Determining the Time of Data Collection 81
    Getting It Done 81

4. Isolate Program Impact 83
    Understanding Why Isolating Impact Is a Key Issue 84
    Applying the Techniques 87
    Building Credibility With the Process 106
    Getting It Done 109

5. Calculate ROI 111
Converting Data to Monetary Value 112
Tabulating Fully Loaded Costs 127
Calculating the ROI 129
Getting It Done 131

6. Optimize Results 133
Telling the Story 134
Developing Reports 140
Data Visualization 150
Using Black Box Thinking to Improve Performance 157
Getting It Done 161

7. Sustain Momentum 163
Identifying Resistance 164
Overcoming Resistance to Implementation 167
Making the ROI Methodology Routine 179
Getting It Done 183

Appendix: ROI Forecasting Basics 189
References 195
Additional Resources 197
About the Authors 203
About ROI Institute 205

About the Training Basics Series

ATD's Training Basics series recognizes and, in some ways, celebrates the fast-paced, ever-changing reality of organizations today. Jobs, roles, and expectations change quickly. One day you might be a network administrator or a process line manager, and the next day you might be asked to train 50 employees in basic computer skills or to instruct line workers in quality processes.

Where do you turn for help? The ATD Training Basics series is designed to be your one-stop solution. The series takes a minimalist approach to your learning curve dilemma and presents only the information you need to be successful. Each book in the series guides you through key aspects of training: giving presentations, making the transition to the role of trainer, designing and delivering training, and evaluating training. The books in the series also include some advanced skills, such as performance and basic business proficiencies. The ATD Training Basics series is the perfect tool for training and performance professionals looking for easy-to-understand materials that will prepare nontrainers to take on a training role.

In addition, this series is the consummate reference tool for any trainer's bookshelf and a quick way to hone your existing skills.

Preface

Consider your most important program—one that is strategic, expensive, high profile, and attracts management attention. Suppose you decide to evaluate the success of the program. Through your analysis you find that participants:
- viewed the program as relevant to their work
- acquired new knowledge and skills
- used the knowledge and skills routinely on the job, although they had some difficulty in a few areas
- improved several important work unit measures, including quality and productivity
- achieved a 105 percent return on the investment in the program
- reported an increase in job satisfaction in their work unit.

From an audience reviewing the data, several questions come to mind. Who and what are the sources of the data? What assumptions are made in the analysis? Is the process consistent from one study to another? Is the study credible? What did it cost to produce the study?

From the program owner's perspective, other questions surface. What would this data mean for your program? What would it mean for your team and you personally? If the above results were negative, what would it mean for the program, your team, and you personally? How should the results be used?

These are the questions faced by hundreds who are beginning their journey into results-based talent development. This book, *ROI Basics*, 2nd edition, will help you answer these questions and understand the true meaning of return on investment (ROI) in talent development.

The Same, Only Better

The ROI Methodology is a comprehensive evaluation process developed in 1973 by Jack J. Phillips. While the five-level evaluation framework is the basis for categorizing data and based on

Preface

Raymond Katzell's four steps of evaluation, the ROI Methodology is the operational process that ensures data collected and categorized within the framework are reliable. More than that, it is a process that enables talent development, and other functions within the organization, to do their job—that is, drive value in the organization. Application of the process is not limited. In fact, the ROI Methodology has reached audiences beyond what we thought it would. Areas in which organizations apply this process include:

- human resources/human capital
- training/learning/development
- leadership/coaching/mentoring
- knowledge management/transfer
- recognition/incentives/engagement
- work arrangement systems
- change management/culture
- talent management/retention
- policies/procedures/processes
- technology/systems/IT
- meetings/events/conferences
- marketing/advertisement/promotion
- compliance/risk management
- organization development/consulting
- project management solutions
- quality/Six Sigma/Lean engineering
- communications/public relations
- public policy/social programs
- creativity/innovation
- ethics/integrity
- safety/health/wellness programs
- environment/sustainability
- healthcare initiatives
- schools/colleges/universities
- public sector/nonprofits
- faith-based programs.

Some of our most exciting work is with nongovernmental organizations, faith-based organizations, and the First Nation community where we are working with the American Indian Fund to demonstrate the value of tribal colleges.

Never before have we seen such interest in designing programs, processes, initiatives, and institutions to drive results that matter to employees, students, stockholders, taxpayers, and communities. The good news is the process to do this hasn't changed—it's the same, only better. Better in terms of the techniques to collect, analyze, report, and optimize data. With greater use, broader adoption, and advances in technology, we continue to learn. We strive to apply that learning by advancing the measurement and evaluation field.

But the fundamentals are the fundamentals—they are foundational and unchanging. They are what makes the ROI Methodology work and why it continues to be the most applied and documented approach to demonstrating impact and ROI for non-capital investments. This book presents those fundamentals. It provides the basics of the ROI Methodology.

What's New

While retaining the fundamentals, this second edition improves on the first, which came out in 2005. The question then is why an update? Because the need for ROI is not going away.

Demonstrating the ROI of programs remains critical to how organizations allocate resources to future programs. Senior executives want to know this information. And yet, we keep hearing the same story: Organizations spend millions of dollars on talent development, but the business measures that matter are not improving! That suggests a continuing gap in connecting how a program performs and whether it delivers value.

Here is what we've changed in this update:
- We have focused more on alignment, as in connecting programs to the business. This includes identifying payoff needs and specific business measures that need to improve. It also includes using a variety of techniques to identify the most feasible solution given the business need.
- While there is so much to talk about on the technology front, we could have written an entire book just on the application and impact of technology on the adoption of the ROI Methodology. Alas, we did not; although, we do give a shout out to a few technologies that are either fundamental tools or new tools that are sure to take measurement to new levels.
- We have also referenced new applications of the process to talent development, demonstrating its increasing use.

What's Inside?

Each chapter provides the basic steps in developing a comprehensive evaluation that includes ROI. Although attempts have been made to address some of the more difficult issues, readers will become most comfortable with the basic techniques. By the end of the book, you will have a basic understanding of the ROI Methodology and be able to select programs for this type of analysis. You will be prepared to develop a strategy to integrate ROI as part of your ongoing talent development process.

Chapter 1, The Basics, provides an overview of ROI—what it means, how it is reported, and when it should be used.

Chapter 2, Plan Your Work, introduces the alignment process, which includes developing program objectives and the evaluation plans that will support your moving forward with an ROI project.

Chapter 3, Collect Data, covers the appropriate data collection procedures and shows how to implement them. This chapter answers the questions: How do you collect data? From whom do you collect data? When do you collect data?

Chapter 4, Isolate Program Impact, addresses one of the most important steps in program evaluation, answering the basic question: How do you know it was your program that improved the measures?

Chapter 5, Calculate ROI, presents the fundamental difference between reporting activity and reporting ROI. It's in the math. Only by converting impact measures to monetary value and comparing that value to the fully loaded cost of the program can an actual ROI be reported.

Chapter 6, Optimize Results, focuses on communicating results and using black box thinking. Without communication, you can't accomplish what you set out to accomplish by evaluating the program. Without reflecting on the wins and losses, and nudging people to take action, you cannot improve the program, the system, or the organization. That's what measurement and evaluation are all about.

Chapter 7, Sustain Momentum, builds on the previous chapter. Anyone can conduct an ROI study, but can you integrate the ROI process into the talent development process so that it is seamless and still effective? This chapter describes how to do that.

The appendix, ROI Forecasting Basics, introduces the concept of forecasting ROI prior to investing in programs, during program implementation, and using Level 3: Application data.

Icons to Guide You

This book has plenty to offer in the way of content that can help you every day. Some icons will alert you to key features of the book.

What's Inside This Chapter

Each chapter opens with a short introduction that serves as a quick reference to the chapter contents. Use this section to identify the information in the chapter and, if you wish, skip ahead to the material that is most useful to you.

Basic Rules
These rules present guiding principles and guidelines to ensure consistent application of the ROI Methodology.

Noted
This icon flags sections with greater detail or an explanation about a concept or a principle. Sometimes it is also used for a short but productive tangent.

Think About This
These considerations attempt to present the information in a slightly different way to reinforce learning as well as to generate an "aha moment" that may not have occurred earlier in the chapter.

Getting It Done
The final section of each chapter supports your ability to take the content of that chapter and apply it to your situation. The focus of this section is mostly on job aids and tools for understanding the content. Sometimes it contains a list of questions for you to ponder, sometimes it is a self-assessment tool, and sometimes it lists action steps you can take to improve your skills and help increase the chances for participant success.

Who Should Read This Book?
The book targets beginners who have been challenged to implement a comprehensive evaluation process as well as those who are taking a proactive approach to accountability. However, those who are more advanced, but still question key issues, will find value in reading this book. Talent development managers will also benefit; by understanding the basics, managers can better serve as champions for ROI implementation.

What Do We Mean?
Before delving into the material, let's clarify a few terms so we're on the same page. *Program* refers to the initiative being evaluated. This could be a course, a full-scale change initiative, or a learning management system implementation. *Talent development* refers to training, performance improvement, learning, development, and education. The *levels of evaluation* refer to the Phillips five-levels

evaluation framework. *ROI* is defined in the true sense of the acronym—earnings divided by investment or net benefits divided by costs.

We hope this book will help you as you move forward with ROI. Best of luck to all of you who do!

Acknowledgments

A book is never developed by the authors alone. It begins with the publisher's willingness to take on the book project and then working with the authors to frame the content in such a way that it will be useful to the target audience. So, our first thanks go to Ann Parker, senior community manager at ATD, for asking us to update the book. We also thank the ATD editorial team for their work in producing the book. ATD has been a long-time partner of ours and we appreciate the opportunity they gave us to lead the measurement and evaluation content for ATD. We believe in the methodology presented here and have observed its successful application in organizations throughout the world. We appreciate ATD's recognition of its importance.

A huge thanks goes to Hope Nicholas, ROI Institute's director of publications. Hope jumped on this book and would not let it (or us) out of her line of sight until it was completed. She always comes through to help us develop quality publications. We would also like to thank our entire team at the ROI Institute who make things happen while we work on research and publications. As other authors will attest, developing a book requires deep work—meaning, we get lost in our work and sometimes come up only when hunger strikes. So many thanks to Ann, Kylie, Sherri, Melissa, Becky, Andy, Brady, and Tim for all you do when we're away!

We'd also like to thank our many workshop participants and clients. Without you, we would have few stories to tell and limited ways in which we could tell them. We appreciate your candor and help in addressing the many issues faced by talent development professionals pursuing this challenging topic.

From Patti to Jack: As always, Jack, you support and encourage me to be my best. I do this by trying to keep up with you! You are my rock, my friend, my love. Thank you!

From Jack to Patti: Much of the success of our work belongs to Patti. She is an outstanding researcher, consultant, teacher, speaker, and author. Her vast knowledge and experience shine through this book. Thank you for the amazing contributions you make each and every day.

All roads lead to ROI!
Patti and Jack Phillips
September 2019

1

The Basics

 What's Inside This Chapter

This chapter explores the fundamentals of the ROI Methodology, a process that has become fundamental to many organizations around the world. The chapter covers three key topics:

- defining return on investment (ROI)
- following the ROI process model
- putting ROI to use.

1

The Basics

Defining ROI

What is ROI? ROI is the ultimate measure of accountability that answers the question: Is there economic value added to the organization for investing in programs, processes, initiatives, and performance improvement solutions? Organizations rely on many economic indicators. Table 1-1 summarizes the typical financial measures important to resource allocation decisions.

Table 1-1. Financial Measures

Financial Measure	Acronym	Description
Return on Investment	ROI	Used to evaluate the efficiency or profitability of an investment or to compare the efficiency of a number of investments. Calculation: Compares the annual net benefits of an investment to the cost of the investment; expressed as a percentage. ROI (%) = (Net Benefits / Costs) x 100
Return on Equity	ROE	Measures a corporation's profitability by revealing how much profit a company generates with the money that shareholders have invested. Used for comparing the profitability of a company to that of other firms in the same industry. Calculation: Compares the annual net income to shareholder equity. ROE = (Net Income / Shareholder Equity) x 100
Return on Assets	ROA	Indicates how profitable a company is in relation to its total assets. Measures how efficient management is at using its assets to generate earnings. Calculation: Compares annual net income (annual earnings) to total assets; expressed as a percentage. ROA (%) = (Net Income / Total Assets) x 100
Return on Average Equity	ROAE	Modified version of ROA referring to a company's performance over a fiscal year. Calculation: Same as ROA except the denominator is changed from total assets to average shareholders' equity, which is computed as the sum of the equity value at the beginning and end of the year divided by two. ROAE = Net Income / Average Shareholder Equity

Financial Measure	Acronym	Description
Return on Capital Employed.	ROCE	Indicates the efficiency and profitability of a company's capital investments. ROCE should always be higher than the rate at which the company borrows; otherwise any increase in borrowing will reduce shareholders' earnings. Calculation: Compares earnings before interest and tax (EBIT) to total assets minus current liabilities. ROCE = EBIT / Total Assets − Current Liabilities
Present Value	PV	Current worth of a future sum of money or stream of cash flows given a specified rate of return. Important in financial calculations including net present value, bond yields, and pension obligations. Calculation: Divides amount of cash flows (C; or sum of money) by the interest rate (r) over a period of time (t). $PV = C / (1 + r)^t$
Net Present Value	NPV	Measures the difference between the present value of cash inflows and the present value of cash outflows. Another way to put it: measures the present value of future benefits with the present value of the investment. Calculation: Compares the value of a dollar today to the value of that same dollar in the future, taking into account a specified interest rate over a specified period of time. $NPV = \sum_{t=1}^{T} (C_t / (1 + r)^t) - C_0$
Internal Rate of Return	IRR	Makes the net present value of all cash flows from a particular project equal to zero. Used in capital budgeting. The higher the IRR, the more desirable it is to undertake the process. Calculation: Follows the NPV calculation as a function of the rate of return. A rate of return for which this function is zero is the internal rate of return. $NPV = \sum_{t=0}^{T} (C_t / (1 + r)^t) - C_0 = 0$
Payback Period	PP	Measures the length of time to recover an investment. Calculation: Compares the cost of a project to the annual benefits or annual cash inflows. PP = Costs / Benefits
Benefit-Cost Ratio	BCR	Used to evaluate the potential costs and benefits of a project that may be generated if the project is completed. Used to determine financial feasibility. Calculation: Compares project annual benefits to its cost. BCR = Benefits / Costs

As shown, each metric compares monetary benefits to costs or investments in some way. Each one has a purpose. Not all metrics, however, are suitable for demonstrating returns gained from non-capital expenditures such as talent development. Instead, three measures can be used for most types of investment, allowing decision makers to use them to compare results across a wide spectrum of programs and projects. The measures are:

- benefit-cost ratio (BCR)
- return on investment (ROI)
- payback period (PP).

The BCR is the output of benefit-cost analysis, an economic theory grounded in welfare economics. As far back as 1667, Sir William Petty, most remembered as a political economist, found that public health expenditures to combat the plague would achieve what is now referred to as a BCR of 84 to 1 (84:1). Later BCR grew in prominence in France with Jules Dupuit's 1844 article on the utility of public works. Economists in the United States adopted BCR in the early 1900s when it was used to justify projects initiated under the River and Harbor Act of 1902 and the Flood Control Act of 1936.

The concept of ROI, comparing earnings to investment, has been used in business for centuries to measure the success of a variety of investment opportunities. *Harvard Business Review*'s 75th anniversary edition in 1997 traced tools used to measure results in organizations (Sibbett 1997). During the 1920s, ROI was the emerging tool to place a value on the payoff of investments. While its initial use was in evaluating the value of capital investments, it has become the leading indicator of value added as a result of human resources and talent development programs. This growth in use for such programs stems, in part, from the 1973 work of Jack J. Phillips who began using it to demonstrate value for a cooperative education program. His use of ROI grew and was formally recorded in his seminal work found in the *Handbook of Training Evaluation and Measurement Methods* (Gulf Publishing, 1983). Over the years, his application of ROI found its way into the broader HR community and has since been adopted across most disciplines.

ROI and BCR provide similar indicators of investment success, though one, ROI, presents the earnings (net benefits) as compared to the cost and is multiplied by 100 to report it as a percentage. The other, BCR, compares gross benefits to costs. Below are the basic formulas used to calculate the BCR and the ROI:

$$BCR = \frac{\text{Program Benefits}}{\text{Program Costs}}$$

$$ROI\ (\%) = \frac{\text{Net Program Benefits}}{\text{Program Costs}} \times 100$$

What does the output of the two formulas mean? A BCR of 2:1 means that for every $1 invested, you receive $2 back. This translates into an ROI of 100 percent, which indicates that for every $1 invested, you receive $1 back after the costs are recovered (you get your investment back plus $1).

BCRs were used in the past primarily in public sector settings, while ROI was used primarily by accountants managing funds in business and industry. Either can be, and are, used in both settings, but it is important to understand the difference. In many cases the BCR and ROI are reported together.

The third measure, payback period (PP), is used to determine the point in time when program owners can expect to recover their investments. Typically, it is used to compare alternative investment opportunities. Those with the shorter PP are usually more desirable. PP does not consider time value of money, nor does it consider future benefits. But it is a simple measure that indicates the break-even point, or a BCR of 1:1, which translates to an ROI of 0 percent. The output of the PP formula is the number of months or years before the projects pay the cost back. The formula for PP is:

$$PP = \frac{\text{Program Costs}}{\text{Program Benefits}}$$

While ROI is the ultimate measure due to it demonstrating the gain over and beyond the costs, basic accounting practice says that reporting the ROI metric alone is insufficient. To be truly meaningful, ROI must be reported with other performance measures.

Periodically, someone will report a BCR of 3:1 and an ROI of 300 percent. This is not possible. ROI is the net benefits divided by the costs, which translates to 200 percent. The net benefit is equal to benefits minus costs.

ROI and the Levels of Evaluation

ROI for talent development programs is reported in the context of the five-level evaluation framework, representing program results important to various stakeholders. These levels are categories of data.

> **Think About This**
>
> A blended learning program led to the reduction in calls escalated from the service desk to field support by an average of 20 per month. The monthly value of this reduction was $175 per call x 20 per month, or $3,500 per month. The first-year benefit of the program was $3,500 x 12, or $42,000. The fully loaded cost for designing, developing, implementing, and evaluating the program was approximately $30,000. Below are the calculations for the BCR, ROI, and PP. Note how, while they tell a similar story, the math and metrics are different.
>
>   BCR = Program Benefits / Program Costs
>   = $42,000 / $30,000
>   = 1.40 or 1.40:1
>
> Translation: For every $1 invested in the program, the organization gained $1.40 in gross benefits.
>
>   ROI (%) = (Net Program Benefits / Program Costs) × 100
>   = ([$42,000 − $30,000] / $30,000) × 100
>   = ($12,000 / $30,000) × 100
>   = 40 percent
>
> Translation: For every $1 invested in the program, the organization recovered its $1 investment and gained an additional $0.40 in net benefit. Or, a 40 percent return over and beyond the investment.
>
>   PP = Program Costs / Program Benefits
>   = $30,000 / $42,000
>   = 0.71 x 12 = 8.57 months
>
> Translation: Given an investment of $30,000 and benefits of $42,000, the organization should recover the program costs within 8.57 months. This suggests that all benefits beyond those gained in 8.57 months will be additional value.

- **Level 1: Reaction and Planned Action**—Data representing participants' reactions to the program and their planned actions are collected and analyzed. Reactions may include participants' views of the course content, facilitation, and learning environment. This category also includes data found to be predictive of application of the acquired knowledge and skills. Such measures include those indicating the participant's perspective of the relevance and importance of the content. Others include the amount of new information presented in the program and participants' willingness to recommend the program to others.
- **Level 2: Learning**—Data representing the extent to which participants acquired new knowledge and skills are collected and analyzed. This category also includes the level of confidence participants have in their ability to apply what they have learned.

- **Level 3: Application and Implementation**—Data are collected and analyzed to determine the extent to which participants effectively apply their newly acquired knowledge and skills. This category also includes data that describes the barriers that prevent application and any supporting elements (enablers) in the knowledge transfer process.
- **Level 4: Impact**—Also referred to as business impact, these data are collected and analyzed to determine the extent to which participants' applications of acquired knowledge and skills positively influenced key measures that were intended to improve as a result of the program. Measures can include both hard and soft data. Hard data are measures of output, quality, cost, and time. Soft data are measures of customer satisfaction, job satisfaction, work habits, and innovation. To ensure credibility and reliability in reporting impact, a step to isolate the program's effects on the improvement in these measures from other influences is always taken.
- **Level 5: Return on Investment**—Impact measures are converted to monetary values and compared with the fully loaded program costs. You may see an improvement in productivity, for example, but the questions remain: What is that improvement worth? How does that value compare to the cost of the program? To calculate an ROI, you must answer these two questions. If the monetary value of productivity's improvement exceeds the cost, your calculation results in a positive ROI.

Noted

The levels of evaluation are categories of data; timing of data collection does not necessarily define the level to which you are evaluating. Level 1 data can be collected at the end of the program (as is typical) or in a follow-up evaluation months after the program (not ideal).

Levels 4 and 5 data can be forecasted before a program is implemented or at the end of the program. The true impact is determined after the program is implemented when actual improvement in key measures can be observed. Through analysis, this improvement is isolated to the program, accounting for other factors. The basics of forecasting ROI are described in the appendix.

Each level of evaluation answers basic questions regarding the program success. Table 1-2 presents these questions along with those associated with the investment itself (Level 0: Input). Level 0 is not a category of results, which is why it is not considered in the five-level framework. But Level 0 data are important, in that they represent how much the organization is investing in

Chapter 1

talent development. Together, these categories of data represent a framework that serves as the basis for assessing, measuring, and evaluating talent development programs.

Table 1-2. Framework of Data and Key Questions

Level of Evaluation	Key Questions
Level 0: Input	• How many people attended the program? • Who were the people attending the program? • How much was spent on the program? • How many hours did it take to complete the program?
Level 1: Reaction and Planned Action	• Was the program relevant to participants' jobs and missions? • Was the program important to participants' jobs and mission success? • Did the program provide new information? • Do participants intend to use what they learned? • Would participants recommend the program to others? • Is there room for improvement with facilitation, materials, and the learning environment?
Level 2: Learning	• Did participants acquire the knowledge and skills presented in the program? • Do participants know how to apply what they learned? • Are participants confident to apply what they learned?
Level 3: Application and Implementation	• How effective are participants at applying what they learned? • How frequently are participants applying what they learned? • If participants are applying what they learned, what is supporting them? • If participants are not applying what they learned, why not?
Level 4: Impact	• So what if the application is successful? • To what extent did application of learning improve the measures the program was intended to improve? • How did the program affect output, quality, cost, time, customer satisfaction, employee satisfaction, and other measures? • How do you know it was the program that improved the measures?
Level 5: Return on Investment	• Do the monetary benefits of the improvement in impact measures outweigh the cost of the program?

The Chain of Impact

Reported together, the levels of data in the framework tell the complete story of program success or failure. Figure 1-1 presents the chain of impact that occurs as organizations invest in talent development programs: participants react positively to those programs; acquire knowledge, skills, information, or insights; and apply that newly acquired knowledge. As a consequence, the application and actions influence key business

Think About This

In 2010, ROI Institute and ATD partnered on a study to determine what measures are most compelling to senior leaders. Impact data ranked first, ROI ranked second, and awards ranked third.

measures. The impact on those measures is known, because a step is taken to isolate the effects of the program from other influences. When these measures are converted to monetary value and compared with the fully loaded program costs, the ROI can be calculated. Because not all impact measures are converted to money, it is important to focus on and report the intangible benefits of the program. Intangible benefits are Level 4 measures not converted to money. So, they do not represent a new "category" of data. Rather, they are noted specifically to complement the ROI metric.

Figure 1-1. Chain of Impact

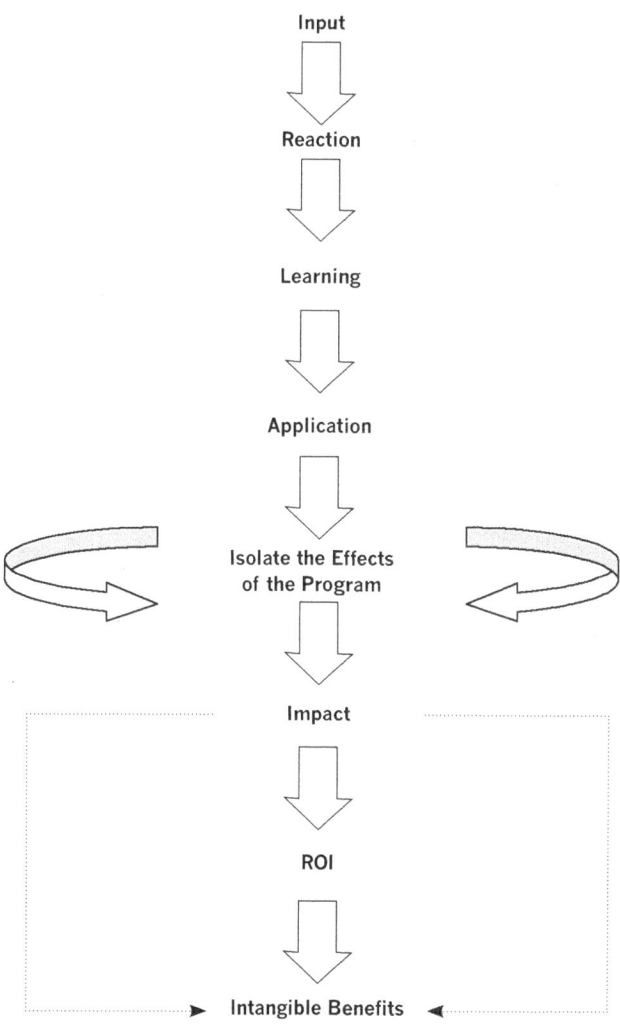

Chapter 1

You may be wondering if it's possible to calculate ROI without the other levels of data. Technically, the answer is, "yes." Each category of data is independent, except for Level 5, which depends on Level 4 measures to start the benefit-cost comparison process. But, if you have a negative or extremely high ROI and you have not collected and analyzed data at the lower levels, how do you explain the results? Together the data in this chain of impact describe a compelling story. As important, it provides the data required to improve programs when the ROI is less than desirable.

The Evaluation Puzzle

To make ROI work, five pieces of an evaluation puzzle must come together, as shown in Figure 1-2. The evaluation framework previously described is the first piece of the puzzle, providing a way to categorize and report data. The second piece is the process model.

Figure 1-2. Evaluation Puzzle

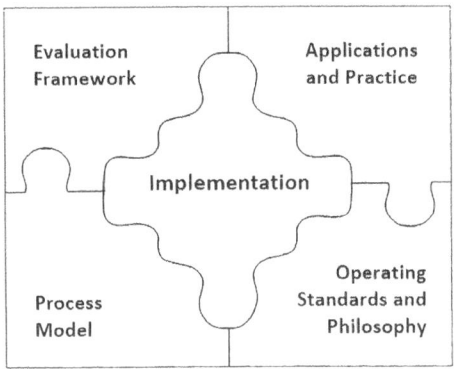

Source: Phillips (2017).

Process Model

The process model serves as a step-by-step guide to help maintain a consistent approach to evaluation. There are four phases to the process, each containing critical steps that must be taken to get to credible information. These four phases are described in more detail later in this chapter:

1. Plan the Evaluation:
   o Align programs with the business.
   o Select the right solution.
   o Plan for results.

2. Collect Data:
   o Design for input, reaction, and learning.
   o Design for application and impact.
3. Analyze Data:
   o Isolate the effects of the program.
   o Convert data to monetary value.
   o Tabulate program costs.
   o Identify intangible benefits.
   o Calculate the ROI.
4. Optimize Results:
   o Communicate results to key stakeholders.
   o Use black box thinking to increase funding.

 Noted

The ROI Methodology was originally developed in 1973 by Jack J. Phillips. Jack, at the time, was an electrical engineer at Lockheed Aircraft (now Lockheed Martin) in Marietta, Georgia, who taught test pilots the electrical and avionics systems on the C-5A Galaxy. He was also charged with managing a co-operative education program designed as part of Lockheed's engineer recruiting strategy. His senior leader told him that in order to continue funding the co-operative education program, Jack needed to demonstrate the return on Lockheed's investment (ROI). The senior leader was not looking for an intangible measure of value, but the actual ROI.

ROI and cost-benefit analysis had been around for decades, if not centuries. But neither had been applied to this type of program. Jack did his research and ran across a concept referred to as four-steps to training evaluation, developed by an industrial-organizational psychologist named Raymond Katzell. Don Kirkpatrick wrote about these steps and cited Katzell in his 1956 article titled "How to Start an Objective Evaluation of Your Training Programs." Because the concept had not been operationalized nor did it include a financial metric describing the ROI, Jack added the economic theory of cost-benefit analysis to the four-step concept and created a model and standards to ensure that reliable data, including the ROI, could be reported to his senior leadership team.

Jack's 1983 *Handbook of Training Evaluation and Measurement Methods* put the five-level evaluation framework and the ROI process model on the map. As he moved up in organizations to serve as head of learning and development, senior executive VP of human resources, and president of a regional bank, he had his learning and talent development and HR teams apply this approach to major programs.

Then, in 1994, his book, *Measuring Return on Investment Volume 1*, published by the American Society of Training & Development (ASTD), now the Association for Talent Development (ATD), became the first book of case studies describing how organizations were using the five-level framework and his process to evaluate talent development programs.

Over the years, Jack Phillips, Patti Phillips, and their team at ROI Institute have authored more than 100 books describing the use of the ROI Methodology. The application of the process expands well beyond talent development and human resources. From humanitarian programs to chaplaincy, and even ombudsmanship, Jack's original work has grown to be the most documented and applied approach to demonstrating value for money of all types of programs and projects.

> **Think About This**
>
> Is your organization large with autonomous divisions? Many organizations pursuing ROI fit this description. If competition exists between divisions, it can lead to divisions purposefully approaching evaluation (and many other things) differently. If each division approaches evaluation, including ROI, using different methodologies and different standards, doesn't it stand to reason that you won't be able to compare the results? Whether it is the approach presented in this book or something else, find a method, develop it, use the standards that support it, and apply it consistently.

Operating Standards and Philosophy

This puzzle piece ensures consistent decision making around the application of the model. Standards provide the guidance needed to support the process and ensure consistent, reliable practice. By following 12 guiding principles, consistent results can be achieved:

1. When conducting a higher-level evaluation, collect data at lower levels.
2. When planning a higher-level evaluation, the previous level of evaluation is not required to be comprehensive.
3. When collecting and analyzing data, use only the most credible sources.
4. When analyzing data, select the most conservative alternative for calculations.
5. Use at least one method to isolate the effects of a project.
6. If no improvement data are available for a population or from a specific source, assume that little or no improvement has occurred.
7. Adjust estimates of improvement for potential errors of estimation.
8. Avoid use of extreme data items and unsupported claims when calculating ROI.
9. Use only the first year of annual benefits in ROI analysis of short-term solutions.
10. Fully load all costs of a solution, project, or program when analyzing ROI.
11. Define intangible measures as measures that are purposely not converted to monetary values.
12. Communicate the results of the ROI Methodology to all key stakeholders.

These guiding principles help maintain a conservative and credible approach to data collection and analysis. They serve as decision-making tools, influencing decisions on the best approach by which to collect data, the best source and timing for data collection, the most appropriate approach for isolation and data conversion, costs to include, and the stakeholders who should receive the results.

Applications and Practice

Applying the ROI Methodology while adhering to the guiding principles is not a simple task, but it does not have to be difficult. Applications and practice, the fourth piece of the evaluation puzzle, provide a deeper understanding of this comprehensive evaluation process. Case application also provides evidence of program success—because without the story, who will know? Thousands of case studies have been developed describing the application of the ROI Methodology. These case studies represent work from business and industry, healthcare, government, and even community and faith-based initiatives.

Professionals who are beginning their pursuit of ROI can learn from these case studies, as well as those found in other publications; however, the best learning comes from actual application. Conducting your own ROI study will allow you to see how the framework, process model, and operating standards come together. It also serves as the starting line for your track record of program success.

Implementation

Conducting just one study adds little value to your efforts to continuously improve and account for your talent development programs. The key is implementation—the last and most critical piece of the evaluation puzzle. Anyone can conduct one ROI study; the key is sustaining the practice. Building the philosophy into everyday decisions about your talent development process is imperative if you want to sustain a culture of results-based talent development. This requires assessing your organization's culture for accountability; assessing your organization's readiness for ROI; defining the purpose for pursuing this level of evaluation; building expertise and capability; creating tools, templates, and standard processes; and adopting technology that will enable optimal use of information that flows from data collection and analysis.

The ROI Process Model

To demonstrate ROI, it is important to follow a step-by-step process to ensure consistent, reliable results. Figure 1-3 presents the ROI Model.

Plan the Evaluation

Planning your ROI evaluation is not only an important first phase in the evaluation process, but an important step in the selection and development of talent development solutions. Without

Figure 1-3. ROI Methodology Process Model

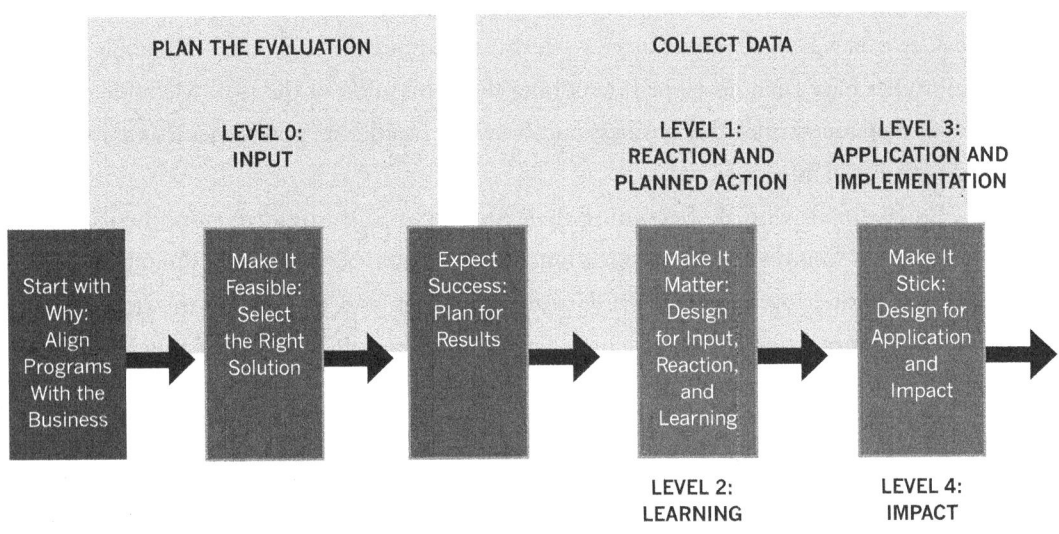

a plan it will be difficult for you to know where you are going, much less when you arrive. Your plan begins with clarifying the business needs for your program and ensuring the most feasible solution has been identified given the needs. Once the correct program has been identified, the next step is to develop specific, measurable objectives and design the program around those objectives. From there you develop your data collection plan. This includes defining the measures for each level of evaluation, selecting the data collection instrument, identifying the source of the data, and determining the timing of data collection. Any available baseline data for the measures you are taking should be collected during this time.

Next, develop the ROI analysis plan. This means selecting the most appropriate technique to isolate the effects of the program on impact data and the most credible method for converting

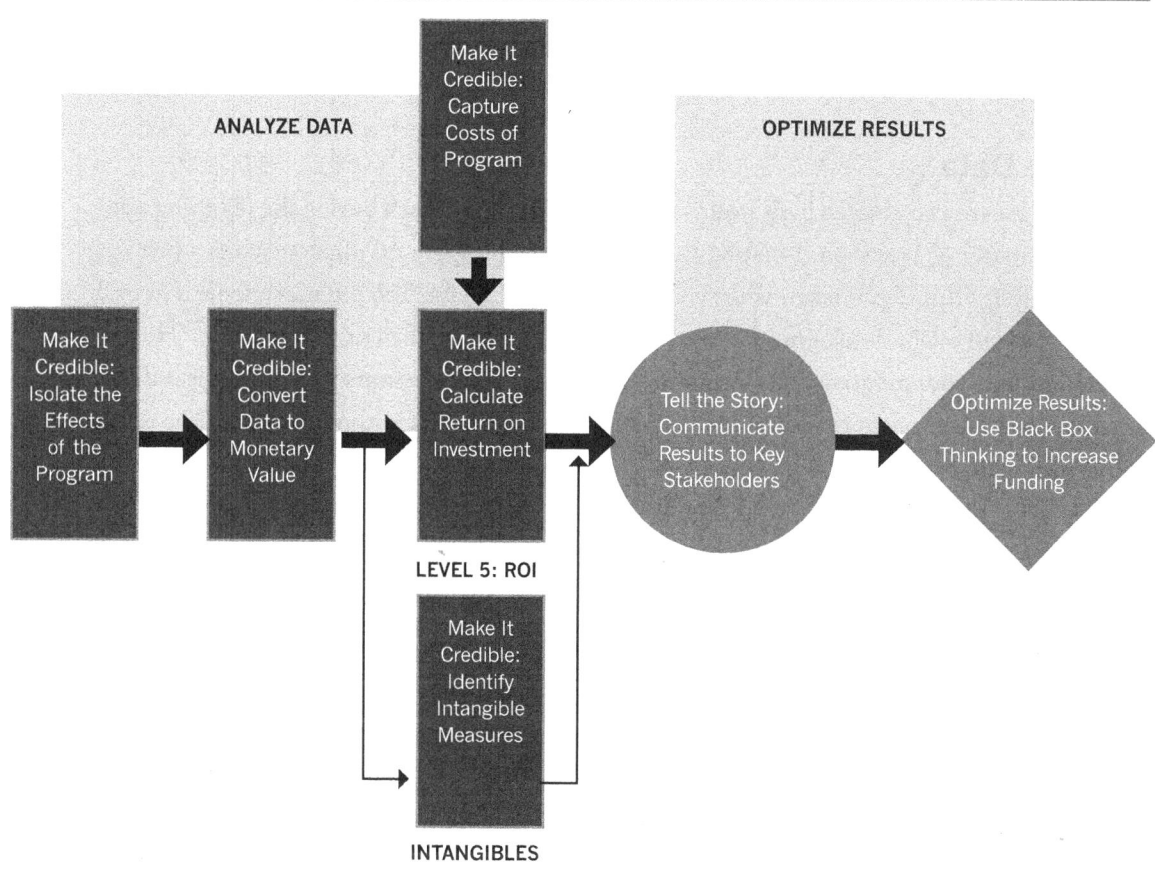

data to money. Cost categories and communication targets are developed. As you develop these planning documents, you will also identify ways in which the evaluation approach can be seamlessly integrated into the program.

Collect Data

Once the planning phase is completed, data collection begins. Levels 1 and 2 data are collected during the program with common instruments, including end-of-course questionnaires, written tests and exercises, and demonstrations. Follow-up data, Levels 3 and 4, are collected sometime after the program when application of the newly acquired knowledge and skills becomes routine and when enough time has passed to observe impact on key measures. A point to remember is that if you have identified the measures that need to improve through initial analysis, you will measure the change in performance in those same measures during the evaluation. It is feasible to believe that your data collection methods during the evaluation could be the same as those used during the needs analysis.

Analyze Data

Once the data are available, analysis begins using the approach chosen during the planning stage. Now it's a matter of execution. Isolating the effects of the program on impact data is a first step in data analysis. This step is taken when collecting data at Level 4. Too often overlooked in evaluating success of talent development programs, this step answers the critical question, "How do you know it was your program that improved the measures?" While some will say this is difficult, we argue (and have argued for years), it doesn't have to be. Besides, without this step, the results you report will lack credibility.

The move from Level 4 to Level 5 begins with converting Level 4: Impact measures to monetary value. Often this step instills the greatest fear in talent development professionals, but once you understand the available techniques to convert data along with the five steps of how to do it (which are covered in chapter 5), the fear usually subsides.

Fully loaded costs are developed during the data analysis phase. These costs include needs assessment (when conducted), design, delivery, and evaluation costs. The intent is to leave no associated cost unreported.

Intangible benefits are also identified during this phase. These are the Level 4 measures not converted to monetary value. They can also represent any unplanned program benefits.

The last step of the data analysis phase is the math. Using simple addition, subtraction, multiplication, and division, the ROI is calculated.

Optimize Results

This is the most important phase in the evaluation process. Evaluation without communication and communication without action are worthless endeavors. If you tell no one how the program is progressing, how can you improve the talent development process, secure additional funding, justify programs, and market programs to future participants?

There are a variety of ways to report data. There are micro reports that include the complete ROI impact study; there are macro reports for all programs that include scorecards, dashboards, and other reporting tools.

But communication must lead to action—and that action requires stepping back and analyzing what is learned from the data. Black box thinking is required if you want to get value from your program evaluation investments. The job of talent development professionals is not to "train" people, but to drive improvement in output, quality, cost, time, customer satisfaction, job satisfaction, work habits, and innovation. This occurs through the development of others; but to do it well, it means assessing, measuring, and evaluating and then taking action based on the findings. Figure 1-4 offers something to remember about the evaluation process.

Figure 1-4. Evaluation Leads to Allocation

Putting ROI to Use

The ultimate use of data generated through the ROI Methodology is to show the value of programs, specifically economic value. But there are a variety of other uses for these data, including to justify spending, improve the talent development process, and gain support.

Justify Spending

Justification of spending is becoming more commonplace in the talent development practice. Talent development managers are often required to justify investing in new programs, the continuation of existing programs, and changes or enhancements to existing programs.

New Programs

In the past, when the talent development function had "deep pockets," new programs were brought on board every time a business book hit the *New York Times* bestseller list. While many of those programs were inspiring, there was no business justification for them. Today, new programs undergo a greater amount of scrutiny. At a minimum, talent development managers consider the costs and provide some esoteric justification for investing the resources.

For those who are serious about justifying investments in new programs, ROI is a valuable tool. A new program's ROI can be forecasted using a variety of techniques, but some programs may require pre-programming justification. There are two approaches for this: pre-program forecasts and ROI in pilot programs. Although these approaches are beyond the scope of this book, the appendix includes basic descriptions of the forecasting techniques.

Existing Programs

Calculating ROI in existing programs is more common in practice than forecasting success for new programs, although there is an increased interest in program justification prior to launch. Typically, ROI is used to justify investments in existing programs where development and delivery have taken place, but there is concern that the value does not justify continuing.

Along with justifying the continuation of existing programs, ROI is used to determine the value of changing delivery mechanisms, such as incorporating blended learning or placing a program online with no in-person interaction. It is also used to justify investing in additional support initiatives that supplement the learning transfer process. Four approaches to ROI can assist in justifying the investment in existing programs: forecasting at Levels 1, 2, and 3, and the post-program evaluation. Post-program evaluation is the basis for this book.

Improve the Talent Development Process

The most important use of ROI is to improve the talent development process. Often talent development staff and program participants are threatened by the thought of being evaluated to such an extent. However, program evaluation is about making decisions concerning the program and the process, not about the individual performance of the people involved. ROI can improve the talent development process by helping staff set priorities, eliminate unsuccessful programs, and reinvent the talent development function.

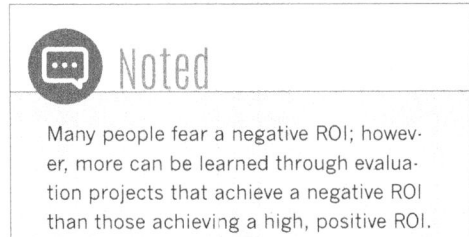

> **Noted**
>
> Many people fear a negative ROI; however, more can be learned through evaluation projects that achieve a negative ROI than those achieving a high, positive ROI.

Set Priorities

In almost all organizations, the need for talent development exceeds the available resources. A comprehensive evaluation process, including ROI, can help determine which programs rank as the highest priority. Programs with the greatest impact (or the potential for greatest impact) are often top priority. Of course, this approach has to be moderated by taking a long view, ensuring that developmental efforts are in place for a long-term payoff. Also, some programs are necessary and represent commitments by the organization. Those concerns aside, the programs generating the greatest impact or potential impact should be given the highest priority when allocating resources.

Eliminate Unsuccessful Programs

You hate to think of eliminating programs—to some people this translates into the elimination of responsibility and, ultimately, the elimination of jobs. This is not necessarily true. For years, the talent development function has had limited tools to eliminate what are known to be unsuccessful, unnecessary programs. ROI provides this tool.

Think About This

Imagine that talent development staff, participants, and participant supervisors know a vendor-supplied customer service program provides little value to the organization. Participants provide evidence of this with their comments on the end-of-course questionnaire. Unfortunately, senior leaders ignore the Level 1 data, asking for stronger evidence that the program is ineffective.

With this edict, the evaluation team sets the course for implementing a comprehensive evaluation. The evaluation results show that in the first year, the program achieved a –85 percent ROI; the second-year forecast shows a slightly less negative ROI of –54 percent. Leaders immediately agree to drop the program.

Sometimes you need to speak the language of business to get your point across.

Reinvent the Talent Development Function

Implementing a comprehensive evaluation process can have many long-term payoffs, one of which is the reinvention of the talent development function. While evaluating to the ROI level is not necessary for all programs, the process itself provides valuable data that can help eliminate unsuccessful programs or reinvent those that are successful but expensive. The funds saved by making these decisions can be transferred to the front-end assessment, resulting in better, more focused programs. This allows for better alignment between talent development and the business, and perpetuates long-term alignment.

Basic Rule 1

Not every program should be evaluated to impact and ROI. ROI is reserved for those programs that are expensive, have a broad reach, drive business impact, have the attention of senior managers, or are highly visible in the organization. However, when evaluation does go to impact and ROI, results should be reported at the lower levels to ensure that the complete story is told.

Chapter 1

Gain Support

A third use for ROI is to gain support for programs and the talent development process. A successful talent development function needs support from key executives and administrators. Showing the ROI for programs can alter managers' and supervisors' perceptions and enhance the respect and credibility of the learning staff.

Key Executives and Administrators

Senior executives and administrators are probably the most important group to the talent development function; they commit resources and show support for functions achieving results that positively affect the strategy of the organization. Known for their support of learning, executives and administrators often suggest training as the solution to every problem. Unfortunately, because training is not always the solution, when the problem persists after the program, executives and administrators can quickly change their thinking. That is why it is common to find talent development absent from high-level decision making.

To ensure talent development's seat at the table, it is necessary for talent development staff and management to think like a business—focusing programs on results and organizational strategy. ROI is one way this focus can occur. Talent development can easily position the function to be a strategic player in the organization by thinking through an opportunity or financial problem that needs to the solved; translating that into the business need; assessing the job performance that needs to be applied to meet the business need; determining the skills necessary to ensure successful job performance; and, finally, deciding the best approach to deliver the knowledge needed to build the skills. ROI evaluation provides the economic justification and value of investing in the mechanism selected to solve the problem.

Managers and Supervisors

Mid-level and frontline supervisors can sometimes be talent development's biggest antagonists. They often question the value of programs because they aren't interested in what their employees learn; rather, they are interested in what employees do with what they learn. Talent development must take learning a step further by showing the effect of what employees do with what they learn, with particular emphasis on measures representative of output, quality, cost, and time. If talent development programs can show results linked to the business and talent development staff can speak the language of business, mid-level managers and supervisors may start to listen to them more closely.

Employees

Showing the value of programs, including ROI, can enhance the talent development function's overall credibility. By showing employees that the programs offered are serious programs achieving serious results, the talent development function can show that training is a valuable way to spend time away from their pressing duties. Also, by making adjustments in programs based on the evaluation findings, employees will see that the evaluation process is not just a superficial attempt to show value.

Getting It Done

It is easy to describe the basics and benefits of using such a comprehensive evaluation process as the ROI Methodology, but this approach is not for everyone. Given that, your first step toward making ROI work for your organization is assessing the degree to which your talent development function is results based. Complete the assessment in Exercise 1-1 to see where you stand. Then ask a client to complete the survey and compare the results.

In the next chapter, you will learn how to create a detailed plan for your evaluation.

Exercise 1-1. Talent Development Program Assessment

Instructions: For each of the following statements, circle the response that best matches the talent development function at your organization.

1. The direction of the talent development function at your organization:
    a. shifts with requests, problems, and changes as they occur
    b. is determined by talent development and adjusted as needed
    c. is based on a mission and a strategic plan for the function

2. The primary mode of operation of the talent development function is to:
    a. respond to requests by managers and other employees to deliver training services
    b. help management react to crisis situations and reach solutions through training services
    c. implement many talent development programs in collaboration with management to prevent problems and crisis situations

3. The goals of the talent development function are:
    a. set by the talent development staff based on perceived demand for programs
    b. developed consistent with talent development plans and goals
    c. developed to integrate with operating goals and strategic plans of the organization

4. Most new programs are initiated:
    a. by request of top management
    b. when a program appears to be successful in another organization
    c. after a needs analysis has indicated that the program is needed

Chapter 1

Exercise 1-1. Talent Development Program Assessment (cont.)

5. When a major organizational change is made you:
    a. decide only which programs are needed, not which skills are needed
    b. occasionally assess what new skills and knowledge are needed
    c. systematically evaluate what skills and knowledge are needed

6. To define talent development plans:
    a. management is asked to choose talent development programs from a list of canned, existing courses
    b. employees are asked about their talent development needs
    c. talent development needs are systematically derived from a thorough analysis of performance problems

7. When determining the timing of training and the target audiences you:
    a. have lengthy, nonspecific talent development training courses for large audiences
    b. tie specific talent development training needs to specific individuals and groups
    c. deliver talent development training almost immediately before its use, and it is given only to those people who need it

8. The responsibility for results from talent development:
    a. rests primarily with the talent development staff to ensure that the programs are successful
    b. is the responsibility of the talent development staff and line managers, who jointly ensure that results are obtained
    c. is a shared responsibility of the talent development staff, participants, and managers all working together to ensure success

9. Systematic, objective evaluation, designed to ensure that participants are performing appropriately on the job, is:
    a. never accomplished; the only evaluations are during the program and they focus on how much the participants enjoyed the program
    b. occasionally accomplished; participants are asked if the training was effective on the job
    c. frequently and systematically pursued; performance is evaluated after training is completed

10. New programs are developed:
    a. internally, using a staff of instructional designers and specialists
    b. by vendors; you usually purchase programs modified to meet the organization's needs
    c. in the most economical and practical way to meet deadlines and cost objectives, using internal staff and vendors

11. Costs for training and talent development are accumulated:
    a. on a total aggregate basis only
    b. on a program-by-program basis
    c. by specific process components, such as development and delivery, in addition to a specific program

12. Management involvement in the talent development process is:
    a. very low with only occasional input
    b. moderate, usually by request, or on an as-needed basis
    c. deliberately planned for all major talent development activities, to ensure a partnership arrangement

13. To ensure that talent development is transferred into performance on the job, you:
    a. encourage participants to apply what they have learned and report results
    b. ask managers to support and reinforce training and report results
    c. use a variety of training transfer strategies appropriate for each situation

14. The talent development staff's interaction with line management is:
    a. rare; you almost never discuss issues with them
    b. occasional; during activities, such as needs analysis or program coordination
    c. regular; to build relationships, as well as to develop and deliver programs

15. Talent development's role in major change efforts is to:
    a. conduct training to support the project, as required
    b. provide administrative support for the program, including training
    c. initiate the program, coordinate the overall effort, and measure its progress—in addition to providing training

16. Most managers view the talent development function as:
    a. a questionable function that wastes too much time of employees
    b. a necessary function that probably cannot be eliminated
    c. an important resource that can be used to improve the organization

17. Talent development programs are:
    a. activity oriented (all supervisors attend the Talent Development Workshop)
    b. individual results based (the participants will reduce their error rate by at least 20 percent)
    c. organizational results based (the cost of quality will decrease by 25 percent)

18. The investment in talent development is measured primarily by:
    a. subjective opinions
    b. observations by management and reactions from participants
    c. dollar return through improved productivity, cost savings, or better quality

19. The talent development effort consists of:
    a. usually one-shot, seminar-type approaches
    b. a full array of courses to meet individual needs
    c. a variety of talent development programs implemented to bring about change in the organization

20. New talent development programs and projects, without some formal method of evaluation, are implemented at your organization:
    a. regularly
    b. seldom
    c. never

21. The results of talent development programs are communicated:
    a. when requested, to those who have a need to know
    b. occasionally, to members of management only
    c. routinely, to a variety of selected target audiences

22. Management involvement in talent development evaluation:
    a. is minor, with no specific responsibilities and few requests
    b. consists of informal responsibilities for evaluation, with some requests for formal training
    c. is very specific. All managers have some responsibilities in evaluation

23. During a business decline at your organization, the talent development function will:
    a. be the first to have its staff reduced
    b. be retained at the same staffing level
    c. go untouched in staff reductions and possibly beefed up

24. Budgeting for talent development is based on:
    a. last year's budget
    b. whatever the training department can "sell"
    c. a zero-based system

25. The principal group that must justify talent development expenditures is:
    a. the talent development department
    b. the human resources or administrative function
    c. line management

Chapter 1

Exercise 1-1. Talent Development Program Assessment (cont.)

26. Over the last two years, the talent development budget as a percentage of operating expenses has:
    a. decreased
    b. remained stable
    c. increased

27. Top management's involvement in the implementation of talent development programs:
    a. is limited to sending invitations, extending congratulations, and passing out certificates
    b. includes monitoring progress, opening and closing speeches, and presentations on the outlook of the organization
    c. includes participating in the program to see what's covered, conducting major segments of the program, and requiring key executives be involved

28. Line management involvement in conducting talent development programs is:
    a. very minor; only talent development specialists conduct programs
    b. limited to a few supervisors conducting programs in their area of expertise
    c. significant; on the average, over half of the programs are conducted by key line managers

29. When an employee completes a talent development program and returns to the job, their supervisor is likely to:
    a. make no reference to the program
    b. ask questions about the program and encourage the use of the material
    c. require use of the program material and give positive rewards when the material is used successfully

30. When an employee attends an outside seminar, upon return, they are required to:
    a. do nothing
    b. submit a report summarizing the program
    c. evaluate the seminar, outline plans for implementing the material covered, and estimate the value of the program

Interpreting the Talent Development Program Assessment
Score the assessment instrument as follows:

- 1 point for each (a) response
- 3 points for each (b) response
- 5 points for each (c) response

Score Range and Analysis

120–150: Outstanding environment for achieving results with talent development. Great management support. A truly successful example of results-based talent development.

90–119: Above average in achieving results with talent development. Good management support. A solid and methodical approach to results-based talent development.

60–89: Needs improvement to achieving desired results with talent development. Management support is ineffective. Talent development programs do not usually focus on results.

30–59: Serious problems with the success and status of talent development. Management support is nonexistent. Talent development programs are not producing results.

2

Plan Your Work

 What's Inside This Chapter

This chapter presents the basics in planning your evaluation:
- aligning programs with the business
- defining program objectives
- developing the evaluation plan.

2

Plan Your Work

Aligning Programs With the Business

While instructional systems design models such as ADDIE (analysis, design, development, implementation, and evaluation) position evaluation at the end, planning for evaluation needs to occur at the beginning—during the analysis phase. This ensures the right measures for evaluation are taken in the end. It leads to a more streamlined and simpler approach to evaluation, not to mention a better program. Evaluation answers the question "why?"

Talent development professionals serve this purpose through their programs and initiatives. To successfully answer the "why," it is important to first align the program with the needs of the organization, and then identify a feasible solution given those needs.

The evaluation framework shown in Table 1-2 serves as the basis for program alignment. By using the five levels to categorize data captured in the analysis phase, talent development professionals can ensure they identify the ultimate needs of the organization as well as the learning needs of the individuals who participate in their programs. This framework is also the basis for defining objectives. As will be presented later in this chapter, objectives serve as the architectural blueprint for a program. Defining objectives at all levels ensures that the program is designed for the results that matter to all stakeholders.

 Noted

"There is nothing so useless as doing efficiently that which should not be done at all."
—Peter Drucker, Austrian-born American management consultant, educator, and author

Figure 2-1 presents the alignment model. As shown on the left, analysis begins with an examination of the payoff opportunities and business needs, and then moves toward the assessment of performance gaps where feasible solutions come to light. Then learning needs are defined, followed by preference needs that answer the question, "How best do we roll out and deliver the content?" Input needs represent the project plan itself (for example, who will participate, how many will participate, what is the cost of delivery). These needs lead to the objectives, which are central to program and evaluation success. They answer the questions "How will we design, develop, and implement the program?" and "How will we measure program success?" The right side of the model represents evaluation, answering the question "What results come from this program?" The measures required to answer this question depend first on clarifying the payoff needs.

Figure 2-1. Alignment Model

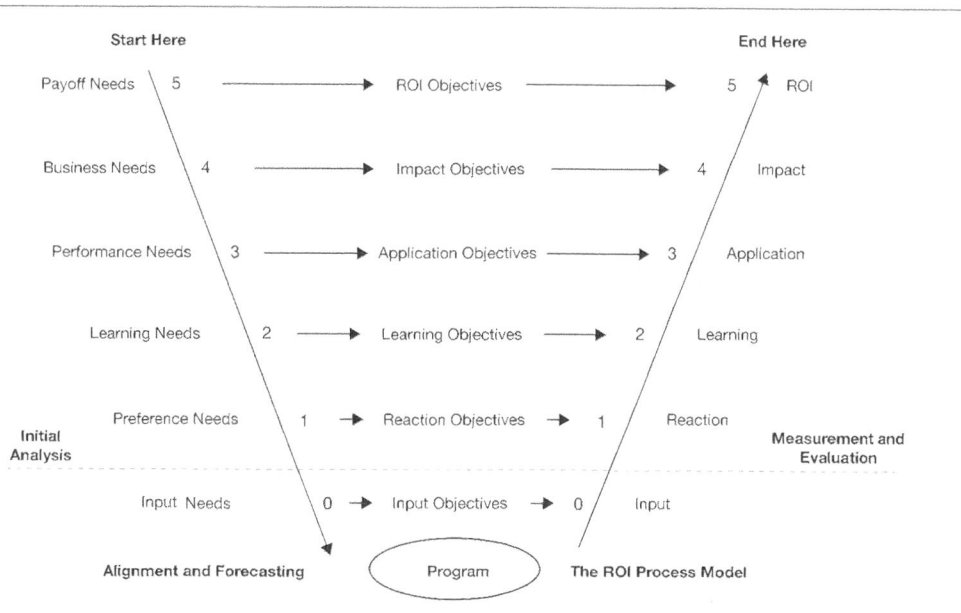

Payoff Needs

Every organization faces opportunities to make money, save money, avoid cost, or contribute to the greater good while making money, saving money, or avoiding cost. Identifying payoff needs is the first step in the alignment process. Payoff needs can be opportunities to pursue or problems to solve. They answer questions such as:
- Is this program worth doing?
- Is the problem worth solving?
- Is the opportunity worth pursuing?

Payoff needs come in the form of profit increase, costs reduction, and cost avoidance. These opportunities are often obvious and relatively easy to connect to monetary values. For example:
- Claim process time has increased 30 percent.
- Our system downtime is double last year's performance.
- The company's safety record is the worst in the industry.
- We have an excessive number of product returns—40 percent higher than last year.

On the other hand, payoff opportunities are sometimes not so obvious, such as:
- Let's implement a team building program.
- We must develop leadership competencies for all managers.
- We need to implement a company-wide cultural transformation initiative.
- It's time to build capability for future growth.

While these seem like admirable goals, the payoff of each is not so clear. To gain clarity, consider the following:
- Why is this an issue?
- What happens if you do nothing?
- Why is this critical?
- How is this linked to strategy?
- What business measures will improve?
- What value will this bring?

Business Needs

While considering the payoff needs, the business needs will often become apparent. Business needs are the specific organizational measures that, if improved, will help address the payoff need. Measures that represent business needs come in the form of output, quality, cost, time, customer satisfaction, job satisfaction, work habits, and innovation.

These measures represent either hard data or soft data. Hard data are objectively based and easily converted to money, for example, citizens vaccinated, graduation rate, loans approved, budget variances, length of stay, cycle time, failure rates, and incidents.

Soft data are subjectively based and, while it is possible, require more effort to convert to money. Examples include teamwork, networking, client satisfaction, organizational commitment, employee experience, creativity, brand awareness, and readiness.

Identifying payoff needs and defining specific business measures up front will help ensure the program targets the right opportunity or addresses the right problem. It also enables easier post-program evaluation.

With payoff and business needs in hand, the next step in the alignment process is to answer the following questions:

- What needs to change to influence the business measures?
- What can enable this change?
- What is the best solution?

Answers to these questions come by assessing performance needs.

Performance Needs

Some talent development professionals are moving from order taker to value creator. These individuals are resisting the temptation to say "yes" to every request for a new program. Rather, they try to uncover the problem or opportunity and identify business measures in need of improvement. Then they identify a solution or solutions that will best influence the business need. Their role is evolving into a performance consulting role, positioning them as critical business partners to leaders throughout the organization.

Success in this movement requires the talent development professional to assess the performance gaps that, if changed, will address business needs. This means they must have a mindset for curiosity and inquiry and be willing to:

- Examine data and records.
- Initiate the discussion with the client.
- Use benchmarking from similar solutions.
- Use evaluation as a hook to secure more information.
- Involve others in the discussion.
- Discuss disasters in other places.
- Discuss consequences of not aligning solutions to the business.

They must also be willing to use, or find others who can use, the wide variety of diagnostics tools available to support this level of needs analysis (see Table 2-1 for some examples).

Table 2-1. Diagnostic Tools to Support Performance Needs Analysis

• Statistical process control	• Force-field analysis	• Diagnostic instruments	• Engagement surveys
• Brainstorming	• Mind mapping	• Focus groups	• Exit interviews
• Problem analysis	• Affinity diagrams	• Probing interviews	• Exit surveys
• Cause-and-effect diagram	• Simulations	• Job satisfaction surveys	• Nominal group technique

Determining which tool or tools to use depends on the scope of the problem or opportunity. An expensive problem warrants comprehensive analysis. For example, at Southeast Corridor Bank (SECOR Bank), the organization was facing customer dissatisfaction and departure, due in part to the inefficiencies in the branches. Analysis of the problem showed that inefficiencies were due to the excessive turnover of bank tellers (71 percent) and the inability of those who remained to serve customer needs. Due to the cost of this problem, leadership decided to invest in a comprehensive performance needs assessment to understand the underlying causes of turnover. One technique employed was the nominal group technique, which involved a series of focus groups with people who represented those who were leaving. SECOR Bank was able to identify 10 reasons why people were leaving the bank and rank them in order of importance (Phillips, Phillips, and Ray 2016). A less expensive problem would have called for a less expensive approach.

This level of analysis usually leads to the most feasible solution or solutions for the business need at hand, with some solutions more obvious than others. In the SECOR Bank study, the team realized it could solve the five most prominent causes of turnover with one solution: a program that would offer training and development opportunities to enable tellers to better serve customers, as well as engage them in the business and with the customers to a greater extent than they had been.

You can use collaborative analytics to discern opportunities to improve output, quality, and cost, as well as employee engagement, customer experience, and other business measures. It is also useful in determining the impact change in collaborative networks has on business measures. While its use is still in its infancy, it is important that talent development professionals become familiar with the opportunities it offers. A good place to begin this learning journey is a research piece authored by Rob Cross, Tom Davenport, and Peter Gray, titled "Driving Business Impact Through Collaborative Analytics" (Connected Commons, April 2019).

Learning Needs

Addressing the performance needs uncovered in the previous step typically requires a learning component to ensure all parties know what they need to do and how to do it. In some cases, a learning program becomes the solution. In other cases, nonlearning solutions such as processes, procedures, policies, and technologies are the most feasible approach to closing the performance gap that will lead to improvement in business measures. Assessing learning needs is not relegated only to pre- and post-knowledge assessments of program participants. Examples of other techniques include: subject matter expert input, job and task analysis, observations, demonstrations, and management assessments.

It is important to go beyond technical knowledge and tactical skill assessment, especially when there is great opportunity at stake. People need to know the "how" as well as the "what," "why," and "when." It is also important to remember that learning needs assessment is important for multiple stakeholders, not just program participants. Supervisors, senior leaders, and the direct reports of the target audience all play a role in ensuring programs are successful.

Preference Needs

Preference needs drive program requirements. Individuals prefer certain content, processes, schedules, or activities for the structure of a program. These preferences inform how best to roll out and deliver a program. If the program is a solution to a problem or if it is leveraging an opportunity, preference needs define how best to implement the program and how participants should perceive it for it to be successful from their perspective. Designing programs based on audience preference increases the odds that participants will commit to them and will be equipped to do what needs to be done to drive the measures that matter.

Input Needs

The last phase of analysis is the project plan, which represents projected investment in the program. Here needs are determined in terms of number of offerings, who will likely participate when, and how many people will participate during each session. The program team will also decide on in-house and external resources to leverage. Travel, food, facilities, and lodging issues are also defined at this stage. At the end of this phase, the program team will estimate the full cost of the program.

The Alignment Model in Action

Table 2-2 presents the output of a basic application of the alignment process. The event that led to this output was a discussion between a chief learning officer (CLO) and the president of operations for a large chip manufacturing company (Phillips and Phillips 2005). The president was concerned that his people spent too much time in training that did not matter. Upon questioning the president, the CLO learned that the concern was not too much training, but rather too much time in meetings in general. She also gained insight into how the meetings were being run and the extent to which follow-through on commitments made in those meetings was taking place. Together they came to an agreement that the president would actively engage in

Table 2-2. Output of Alignment Process

Level of Need	Needs
Payoff Needs	What is the economic opportunity or problem? • Specific dollar amount is unknown. Estimate thousands in U.S. dollars due to time wasted in meetings.
Business Needs	What are the specific business needs? • Too many meetings (frequency of meetings per month) • Too many people attending meetings (number of people per month) • Meetings are too long (average duration of meetings in hours)
Performance Needs	What is happening or not happening on the job that is causing this issue? • Meetings are not planned • Agendas are not developed prior to the meeting • Agendas are not being followed • Consideration of the time and cost of unnecessary meetings is lacking • Poor facilitation of meetings • Follow-up action resulting from the meeting is not taking place • Conflict that occurs during meetings is not being appropriately managed • Proper selection of meeting participants is not occurring • Good meeting management practices are not implemented • Consideration of cost of meetings is not taking place
Learning Needs	What knowledge, skill, or information is needed to change what is happening or not happening on the job? • Ability to identify the extent and cost of meetings • Ability to identify positives, negatives, and implications of meeting issues and dynamics • Effective meeting behaviors
Preference Needs	How best can this knowledge, skill, or information be communicated so that change on the job occurs? • Facilitator-led workshops • Job aids and tools • Relevant and useful information is required
Input Needs	What is the projected investment? • 72 supervisors and team leaders who lead meetings • Average salary $219 per day • Break out in three groups • Two-day workshop for all 72 people • Program fee for 72 people (includes facilitations and materials) • Estimated travel and lodging • Cost of facilities for six days (2 days x 3 offerings) • Prorated cost of needs assessment • Estimated cost of evaluation (≈5% program cost) • Estimated cost: $125,000

supporting learning transfer in an effort to reduce the cost of spending too much time in meetings. They also agreed that the cost reduction would exceed the cost of solution implementation, targeting an ROI of 25 percent. This would indicate to the president that for every $1 invested in the solution, the organization would gain an additional $0.25.

> **Think About This**
>
> Sometimes it is important to forecast the ROI for a program prior to investing in it; for example, if the program is very expensive or when deciding between different delivery mechanisms. Pre-program forecasting is also important when deciding between two programs intended to solve the same program. The appendix includes a basic description of pre-program forecasting as well as descriptions of how to forecast ROI with data representing the other levels of evaluation.

Defining Program Objectives

Program objectives represent the expectation for success. More importantly, they serve as the architectural blueprint that talent development professionals should follow if they want to design programs for results. They answer the question, "How?" meaning, "How will we design, develop, and implement this program?" and "How will we measure the program's success?"

Program objectives reflect the same framework used in categorizing evaluation data. The key in writing program objectives is to be specific in identifying measures of success and to ensure that the measures align with those discovered through the needs assessment. All too often, broad program objectives are written or the measures that define those objectives are irrelevant to the need for the program. Vague and irrelevant objectives hurt the design of the program, impair the evaluation process, and lead to meaningless results.

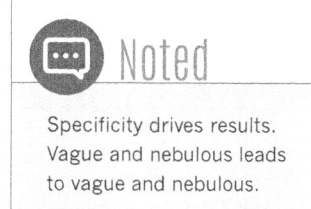
> **Noted**
>
> Specificity drives results. Vague and nebulous leads to vague and nebulous.

Level 1: Reaction and Planned Action Objectives

Level 1 objectives are critical in that they describe expected immediate and long-term satisfaction with a program. They describe issues important to the success of the program, including facilitation, relevance and importance of content, logistics, and intended use of knowledge and skills. But there has been criticism of the Level 1 evaluation surrounding the use of the Level 1 overall satisfaction as a measure of success. Overuse of the overall satisfaction measure has led many organizations to make funding decisions based on whether participants like a program; later, they realize the data were misleading.

Level 1 objectives should identify issues that are important and measurable rather than esoteric indicators that provide limited useful information. They should be attitude based, clearly worded, and specific. Level 1 objectives specify whether the participant has had a change in thinking or perception as a result of the program and underscore the linkage between attitude and the program's success. While Level 1 objectives represent a satisfaction index from the consumer perspective, these objectives should also have the capability to predict program success. Given these criteria, it is important that Level 1 objectives represent specific measures of success. A good predictor of the application of knowledge and skills is the perceived relevance by participants of program content. So, a Level 1 objective may be:

> At the end of the course, participants will perceive program content as relevant to their jobs.

A question remains, however: "How will you know you are successful with this objective?" This is where a good measure comes in. Table 2-3 compares a broad objective with a more specific measure.

Table 2-3. Compare Broad Objective With More Specific Measure

Objective	Measure
At the end of the course, participants will perceive program content as relevant to their jobs.	• 80 percent of participants rate program relevance a 4.5 out of 5 on a Likert scale.

For those of you who are more research driven, you might want to take this a step further by defining (literally) what you mean by "relevance." For example, relevance may be defined as:
- knowledge and skills that participants can immediately apply in their work
- knowledge and skills that reflect participants' day-to-day work activity.

Now the measures of success can be even more detailed. Table 2-4 compares the broad objective to the more detailed measures. Success with these two measures can be reported individually, or you can combine the results of the two measures to create a "relevance index."

Table 2-4. Compare A Broad Objective With More Specific and Detailed Measures

Objective	Measures
At the end of the course, participants will perceive program content as relevant to their jobs.	• 80 percent of participants indicate that they can immediately apply the knowledge and skills in their work as indicated by a 4.5 rating out of 5 on a Likert scale. • 80 percent of participants view the knowledge and skills as reflective of their day-to-day work activity as indicated by rating this measure a 4.5 out of 5 on a Likert scale.

Breaking down objectives to multiple, specific measures provides a clearer picture of success; however, multiple measures also lengthens your Level 1 data collection instrument. The question to consider is, "Do you need a long questionnaire with many questions representing many measures to determine success with an objective?" For a program planned for ROI evaluation, no. Keep your lower-level evaluation instruments simple (yet, meaningful) when planning an evaluation that includes impact and ROI. Conserve your resources for the more challenging tasks of Level 4 and Level 5 evaluation.

 Think About This

Overall satisfaction is sometimes referred to as a measure of how much participants liked the program's snacks. Recent analysis of a comprehensive Level 1 end-of-course questionnaire showed that participants viewed the program as less than relevant and not useful, and had little intention to use what they learned. Scores included:
- Knowledge and skills presented are relevant to my job: 2.8 out of 5.
- Knowledge and skills presented will be useful to my work: 2.6 out of 5.
- I intend to use what I learned in this course: 2.2 out of 5.

Surprisingly, however, respondents scored the overall satisfaction measure, "I am satisfied with the program," as 4.6 out of 5. Hmm, it must have been the cookies!

Level 2: Learning Objectives

There is ongoing interest in evaluating the acquisition of knowledge and skills. These drivers include growth in the number of learning organizations, placing emphasis on intellectual capital, and increased use of certifications as discriminators in the selection process. Given this, Level 2 objectives should be well defined.

Level 2 objectives communicate expected outcomes from instruction; they describe competent performance that should be the result of learning. The best learning objectives describe behaviors that are observable and measurable. As with Level 1 objectives, Level 2 objectives are outcome based. Clearly worded and specific, they spell out what the participant must be able to do as a result of learning.

Basic Rule 2

When conducting a higher-level evaluation, collect data at lower levels.

There are three types of learning objectives:
- **Awareness**—participants are familiar with terms, concepts, and processes.

- **Knowledge**—participants have a general understanding of concepts and processes.
- **Performance**—participants are able to demonstrate the knowledge and skills acquired.

A typical learning objective may be:

> At the end of the course, participants will be able to use Microsoft Word.

Sounds reasonable. But what does "successful use" look like? How will you know if you have achieved success? You need a measure, as shown in Table 2-5. Now, you can evaluate the success of learning.

Table 2-5. Compare Broad Objective With Implementation Measures

Objective	Measures
At the end of the course, participants will be able to use Microsoft Word.	Within a 10-minute time period, participants will be able to demonstrate to the facilitator the following applications of Microsoft Word with zero errors: • File, save as, save as web page • Format, including font, paragraph, background, and themes • Insert tables, add columns and rows, and delete columns and rows

Level 3: Application and Implementation Objectives

Where learning objectives and their specific measures of success tell you what participants can do, Level 3 objectives tell you what participants are expected to do when they leave the learning environment. Application objectives describe the expected outputs of the talent development program, which include competent performance resulting from training, and provide the basis for evaluating on-the-job performance changes. The emphasis is placed on applying what was learned.

The best Level 3 objectives identify behaviors that are observable and measurable; they are outcome based, clearly worded, specific, and spell out what the participant has changed as a result of the learning. A typical application objective might read something like:

> Participants will use effective meeting behaviors.

Again, you need specifics to evaluate success. What are effective meeting behaviors and to what degree should participants use those skills? Some examples of measures are shown in Table 2-6. With defined measures, you now know what success looks like.

An important element of Level 3 evaluation is that this is where you assess success with learning transfer. Is the system supporting learning? Here you look for barriers to application and supporting elements (enablers). It is critical to gather data around these issues so that you can take corrective action when evidence of a problem exists. You may wonder how you can influence issues outside your control—say, when participants indicate that their supervisor is preventing them from applying newly acquired knowledge. Through the evaluation process, you can collect data that arm you to engage in dialogue with supervisors. Bring the supervisors into the fold and ask them for help. Tell them there is evidence that some supervisors are not supporting learning opportunities and you need their advice as how to remedy the situation.

Table 2-6. Compare Application Objective With Measurable Behaviors

Objective	Measures
Participants will use effective meeting behaviors.	• Participants will develop a detailed agenda outlining the specific topics to be covered for 100 percent of meetings. • Participants will establish meeting ground rules at the beginning of 100 percent of meetings. • Participants will follow up on meeting action items within three days following 100 percent of meetings.

A comprehensive assessment at Level 3 provides you with tools to begin this dialogue with all stakeholders. Through it you may find that many managers, supervisors, and colleagues in other departments don't understand the role of talent development, nor do they have a clear understanding of the adult learning process. This is an opportunity to teach them, and thereby, increase their support.

Level 4: Impact Objectives

Success with Level 4 objectives is critical when you want to achieve a positive ROI for the talent development investment. Level 4 objectives provide the basis for measuring the consequences of application of skills and knowledge and place emphasis on achieving bottom-line results. The best impact measures are both linked to the knowledge and skills in the program and easily collected. Level 4 objectives are results based, clearly worded, and specific. They spell out what the participant has accomplished in the business unit as a result of the program. Four types of impact objectives involving hard data are output focused, quality focused, cost focused, and time focused. Three common types of impact measures involving soft data are customer service focused, work climate focused, and work habit focused.

Say you work for a large, multinational computer manufacturer that prides itself on the quality of the computer systems purchased and the service provided when there is a problem. The company makes it easy for purchasers to get assistance by selling lucrative warranties on all its products. One particular system, the X-1350, comes with a three-year warranty that includes the "gold standard" for technical support for an additional $105.

In the past year, there has been an increase in the number of call-outs to repair contractors, particularly with regard to the X-1350. This increase is costing the company not only money, but also customer satisfaction. A new program is implemented to improve the computer's quality. A typical impact objective might read something like:

However, that objective is too broad. To determine if your efforts will have their intended impact, focus your impact measure on specific measures—in this example, measures of quality. Table 2-7 shows the objective and specific measures of success.

Table 2-7. Compare Broad Objective With Impact Measures

Objective	Measure
Improve the quality of the X-1350.	• Reduce the number of warranty claims on the X-1350 by 10 percent within six months after the program. • Improve overall customer satisfaction with the quality of the X-1350 by 10 percent as indicated by a customer satisfaction survey taken six months after the program. • Achieve top scores on product quality measures included in industry quality survey.

Specific measures describe the meaning of success. They also serve as the basis for the questions that you ask during the evaluation.

Level 5: ROI Objectives

Level 5 objectives target the specific economic return anticipated when an investment is made in a program. This objective defines "good" when asked, "What is a good ROI?" There are four options when considering the target ROI:

- Set the ROI at the level of other investments.
- Set the ROI at a higher standard.
- Set the ROI at break-even.
- Set the ROI based on client expectations.

Set ROI at the Level of Other Investments

Setting ROI at the same level as other investments is not uncommon. Many talent development groups use this approach to ensure a link with operations. To establish this target, ask your finance and accounting teams what the average return is for other investments.

Set ROI at a Higher Standard

Another approach to establishing the Level 5 objectives is to raise the bar for talent development. Set the target ROI at a higher level than the other investments. Because talent development affects so many and contributes so much to the organization, a higher than normal expected ROI is not unreasonable.

Set ROI at Break-Even

Some organizations are satisfied with a 0 percent ROI—break-even. This says that the organization got the investment back. For instance, if an organization spends $50,000 on a particular program, the monetary benefit was $50,000—there was no gain beyond the investment return, but the investment came back. Many organizations, such as nonprofit, community-, and faith-based organizations value break-even ROI.

Set ROI Based on Client Expectations

A final strategy to setting the Level 5 objective is to ask the client. Remember that the client is the person or group funding the program. They may be willing to invest in a program given a certain return on that investment.

Developing the Evaluation Plan

There are two basic documents that you will complete when planning your ROI impact study. These are the data collection plan and the ROI analysis plan. By completing these plans thoroughly, you will be well on your way to conducting an ROI study. Once completed, have the client sign off on your approach to the evaluation. By taking this important step, you gain buy-in and the confidence of knowing that you have support for your planned approach. But before you set off on planning the actual ROI study, it is important to clarify the purpose and feasibility of pursuing such a comprehensive evaluation. Yes, the needs assessment may align the program with key impact measure that, if improved, will lead to a payoff, but is the program really suitable for impact and ROI evaluation?

Chapter 2

Purpose

Purpose keeps you focused on the "why" of the evaluation. This provides a basis for using the data once generated. All too often, evaluation is done without understanding the purpose of the process; therefore, you let the raw data sit for days, months, and sometimes years before you consider analyzing it to see what happened.

Defining the purpose of the evaluation helps determine the scope of the evaluation project. It drives the type of data to be collected as well as the type of data collection instruments to be used.

Evaluation purposes range from demonstrating the value of a particular program to boosting credibility for the entire talent development function. Typical evaluation purposes can be categorized into three overriding themes:

- making decisions about programs
- improving programs and processes
- demonstrating program value.

Making Decisions About Programs

Decisions are made every day, with and without evaluation data. But, with evaluation data, the talent development function can better influence those decisions. Evaluation data can help you make decisions about a program prior to its launch, for example, when you forecast the ROI in a pilot program. Once you know the results of the evaluation, you can decide whether to pursue the program further.

Evaluation data can help the talent development staff make decisions about internal development issues. For example, Level 1 data provide information that helps determine the extent to which facilitators need additional skill building. Level 2 data can help you decide whether an additional exercise will better emphasize a skill left undeveloped. Level 3 data not only tell supervisors the extent to which their employees are applying new skills, but also the extent to which events under their control are preventing employees from applying the skills. Data from Levels 4 and 5 help senior managers and executives decide whether they will continue investing in certain programs.

Decisions are made with or without evaluation data. By providing data, the talent development team can influence the decision-making process.

The levels of evaluation provide different types of data that influence different decisions. Table 2-8 presents a list of decisions that evaluation data, including ROI, can influence.

Table 2-8. Decisions Made With Evaluation Data

Decision	Level of Evaluation
Talent development staff want to decide whether they should invest in skill development for facilitators.	Level 1
Course designers are concerned the exercises do not cover all learning objectives and need to decide which skills need additional support.	Level 2
Supervisors are uncertain as to whether they want to send employees to future training programs.	Levels 3 and 4
The clients of the talent development team are deciding if they want to invest in expanding a pilot leadership program for the entire leadership team.	Level 5
Senior managers are planning next year's budget and are concerned about allocating additional funding to the talent development function.	Levels 1–5 (scorecard)
The talent development staff are deciding whether they should eliminate an expensive program that is getting bad reviews from participants, but a senior executive plays golf with the training supplier.	Level 5
A training supplier is trying to convince the talent development team that their leadership program will effectively solve the turnover problem.	Level 5 (forecast/pilot)
Supervisors want to implement a new initiative that will change employee behavior because they believe the talent development program did not do the job.	Level 3 (focus on barriers and enablers)

Improving Programs and Processes

One of the most important purposes in generating comprehensive data using the ROI Methodology is to improve talent development programs and processes. As data are generated, the programs being evaluated can be adjusted so that future presentations are more effective. Reviewing evaluation data in the earlier stages allows the talent development function to implement additional tools and processes that can support the transfer of learning.

Evaluation data can help the talent development function improve its accountability processes. By consistently evaluating programs, the talent development function will find ways to develop data more efficiently through technology or through the use of experts within the organization. Evaluation will also cause the talent development staff to view its programs and processes in a different light, asking questions such as, "Will this prove valuable to the organization?" "Can we get the same results for less cost?" "How can we influence the supervisors to better support this training program?"

Demonstrating Program Value

A fundamental purpose of conducting comprehensive evaluation is to show the value of talent development programs—specifically, the economic value. But when considering individual programs you plan to evaluate, you often have to ask yourself "value to whom?"

Value is not simply defined. Just as learning occurs at the societal, community, team, and individual levels, value is defined from the perspective of the stakeholder:

- Is a program valuable to those involved?
- Is a program valuable to the system that supports it?
- Is a program economically valuable?

Value can be defined from three perspectives. These perspectives are put into context by comparing them to the five-level evaluation framework. Table 2-9 presents these perspectives. The consumer perspective represents the extent to which those involved in the program react positively and acquire some level of knowledge and skills as a result of participating. The system perspective represents the supporting elements within the organization that make the program work. The economic perspective represents the extent to which knowledge or skills transferred to the job positively affect key business measures; when appropriate, these measures are converted to monetary value and compared with the cost of the program to calculate an economic metric, ROI.

Table 2-9. Value Perspectives

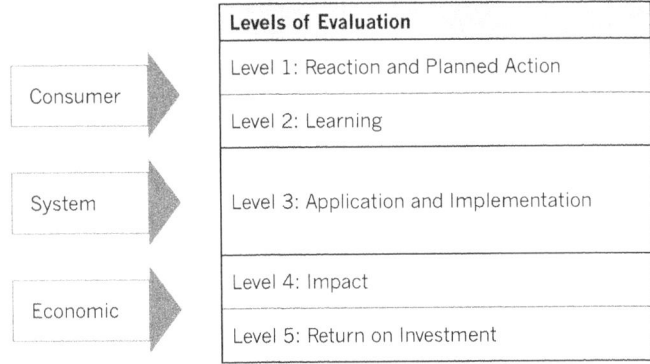

	Levels of Evaluation
Consumer	Level 1: Reaction and Planned Action
	Level 2: Learning
System	Level 3: Application and Implementation
Economic	Level 4: Impact
	Level 5: Return on Investment

Consumer Perspective

The consumers of talent development are those who have an immediate connection with the program. Facilitators, designers, developers, and participants represent consumers. Value to this group is represented at Levels 1 and 2. Data provide the talent development staff feedback so they can make immediate changes to the program as well as decide where developmental needs exist. These data provide a look at what the group thought about the program and how they each fared from a knowledge and skills acquisition perspective compared to the group. Some measures—

those representing utility of knowledge gain—are often used to predict actual application of knowledge and skills.

System Perspective

The system represents those people and functions that support learning within an organization. This includes participant supervisors, participant peers and team members, executives, and support functions, such as the IT department or the talent development function. In many cases, the system is represented by the client.

Although Level 3 data provide evidence of participant application of newly acquired knowledge and skills, the greatest value in evaluating at this level is in determining the extent to which the system supports learning transfer. This is determined by the barriers and enablers identified through the Level 3 evaluation.

Economic Perspective

The economic perspective is typically that of the client—the person or group funding the program. Although the supervisor will be interested in whether the program influenced business outcomes and the ROI, it is the client—who is sometimes the supervisor, but more often senior management—who makes the financial investment in the program. Levels 4 and 5 provide data representing the economic value of the investment.

Table 2-10 presents the value perspectives compared with the frequency of use of the data provided by each level of evaluation. Although there is value at all levels, the lower levels of evaluation are implemented most frequently and tend to be of greater value to clients. This is due to the feasibility of conducting evaluations at the lower levels versus the higher levels.

Table 2-10. Value Perspective Versus Use

	Levels of Evaluation	Value of Information	Customer Focus	Frequency of Use	Difficulty of Assessment
		Least	Participants	Frequent	Easy
Consumer	Level 1: Reaction and Planned Action				
Consumer	Level 2: Learning				
System	Level 3: Application and Implementation				
Economic	Level 4: Impact				
Economic	Level 5: Return on Investment				
		Greatest	Client	Infrequent	Difficult

Feasibility

Program evaluations have multiple purposes—when you evaluate at Level 5 to influence funding decisions, you still need Level 1 data to help you improve delivery and design. This is one reason the lower levels of evaluation are conducted more frequently than the higher levels. Other drivers that determine the feasibility of evaluating programs to the various levels include the program objectives, the availability of data, and the appropriateness for ROI.

Program Objectives

As described earlier, program objectives are the basis for evaluation. Program objectives drive the design and development of the program and show how to measure success. They define what the program is intended to do, and how to measure participant achievement and system support of the learning transfer process. All too often, however, minimal emphasis is placed on developing objectives and their defined measures at the higher levels of evaluation.

Availability of Data

A question to consider is "Can you get the information you need to determine if the objectives are met?" The availability of data at Levels 1 and 2 is rarely a concern. Simply ask for the opinion of the program participants, test them, or facilitate role plays and exercises to assess their overall knowledge, skills, and insight. Level 3 data are often obtained by going to participants, their supervisors, their peers, and their direct reports. The challenge is in the availability of Level 4 data. While the measures are typically monitored on a routine basis, the question is often how the talent development team can access them. The first step is to determine where they are housed, and then build a relationship such that the owners of the measures will partner with you so you can access the data you need. Occasionally, reliance on participants to provide information on the measures is the best approach. But if they are not the right audience, how will they access the data?

Program objectives and data availability are key drivers in determining the feasibility of evaluating a program to ROI; however, some programs are just inappropriate for ROI.

Appropriateness for ROI

How do you know if a program is appropriate for ROI evaluation? By answering the following questions:

- What other factors will influence improvement in the business measures?
- How will you isolate the effects of your program on improvement in the impact measures from other influences?
- Can impact measures be converted to monetary value given cost constraints and so that the value is perceived as credible?
- Does the profile of the program meet specific criteria?

The first two questions represent the most important, yet, most misunderstood step in the ROI process—isolating the effects of the program. Talent development professionals will sometimes question the feasibility and appropriateness of this step. But, if you report business impact or ROI in programs without taking this step, the information will be invalid. If you suggest that your sales program generated enough profit to overcome the costs of the program resulting in a 50 percent ROI, someone in the organization will ask, "How do you know your sales training program was what generated that profit?"

There are a variety of ways to isolate the effects of programs, which are described in chapter 4. Control group methodology is one; however, while it's the gold standard of techniques, it is often the least feasible. If you do not intend to take this step in the process, then don't report business impact or ROI. You'll set yourself up to lose credibility.

The next question is fundamental in moving from Level 4 to Level 5—converting data to monetary value. Omit this step, and you cannot report ROI. As discussed earlier, ROI is an economic indicator comparing the monetary benefits of a program to the fully loaded costs. If you cannot convert a measure to monetary value given the cost constraints under which you are working or so that it is perceived as a credible value, report the improvement as intangible (still an important benefit, just not one that will be included in the ROI calculation).

There are a variety of ways to calculate monetary value for impact measures including standard values, historical costs, expert opinion, estimations, and previous studies. (Read chapter 5 for more information.) The key is converting the measure given cost constraints and so stakeholders perceive the value as credible.

 Noted

Not all programs are suitable for impact and ROI evaluation; but when you do evaluate to these levels, use at least one method to isolate the effects of the program and credibly convert data to monetary value.

The last question to consider in assessing the appropriateness of a program in going to ROI is the program profile—does it meet specific criteria? An inexpensive program offered one time, never to be offered again, is not suitable for ROI. Why invest resources in conducting such a comprehensive evaluation on a program for which the data serve no valuable or ongoing purpose? Basic skill building is not always suitable for ROI, for example, a program for basic computer skills. Sometimes you just want to know that participants know how to do something rather than what the impact of their doing it has on key business measures. Induction programs are not always suitable for ROI, especially entry-level programs in which participants are just beginning their professional careers.

So what programs are suitable for ROI? Those programs that are:

- expected to have a long life cycle
- linked to organization strategy
- connected to organization objectives
- expensive, requiring resources, time, and money
- targeted to a large audience
- highly visible throughout the organization
- of interest to management
- intended to drive major change within the organization.

Table 2-11 presents targets based on a benchmarking study of users of the ROI Methodology. These targets can serve as a guide in developing your evaluation strategy.

Table 2-11. Percentage of Programs Evaluated at Each Level

	Level 1	Level 2	Level 3	Level 4	Level 5
Targets	90–100%	60–90%	30–40%	10–20%	5–10%

Data Collection Plan

The data collection plan lays the initial groundwork for the ROI study. This plan holds the answers to the questions:

- What do you ask?
- How do you ask?
- Whom do you ask?
- When do you ask?
- Who does the asking?

What Do You Ask?

The answers to this question lie in the program objectives and their respective measures. Specific measurable objectives and measures of success serve as the basis for the questions you intend to ask. When broad objectives are developed, the measures must be clearly described so that you know when success is achieved.

How Do You Ask?

How you ask depends on a variety of issues, including resources available to collect data. Level 1 data are typically collected using the end-of-course questionnaire. To collect Level 2 data, use tests, role plays, self-assessments, demonstrations and simulations, or peer and facilitator assessments. Follow-up data collection (Levels 3 and 4) is the most challenging; however, there are a variety of options, including questionnaires, focus groups, interviews, action plans, and performance monitoring. These options provide flexibility and ensure that the lack of data collection methods is not a barrier to following up on program application and impact.

Whom Do You Ask?

Your source of data is critical. You will go only to the most credible source; sometimes this includes multiple sources. The more sources providing data, the more reliable the data. The only condition is the cost of going to those multiple sources.

When Do You Ask?

Timing of data collection is critical and getting it right can be a challenge. You want to wait long enough for new behaviors to have had time to become routine, but not so long that the participants forget how they developed the new behavior. You also want to wait long enough for impact to occur, but most executives aren't willing to wait an extended period of time. Therefore, you have to pick a point in time at which you believe application and impact have occurred. Timing, just like the measures themselves, should be defined during the development of the program objectives and based on the needs of the organization.

Who Does the Asking?

Who will be responsible for each step in the data collection process? Typically, the facilitator collects data at Levels 1 and 2. For the higher levels of evaluation, representatives of the evaluation team are assigned specific roles. One of these roles is data collection. A person or team is assigned to the task of developing the data collection instrument and administering it. This includes developing a strategy to ensure a successful response rate.

Table 2-12 presents an example of a completed data collection plan.

ROI Analysis Plan

The second planning document is the ROI analysis plan, which requires that you identify:

- methods for isolating the effects of the program
- methods for converting data to monetary value
- cost categories
- intangible benefits
- communication targets for the final report
- other influences and issues during application
- comments.

The ROI analysis plan also includes a column for comments or any notes that you might need to take regarding the evaluation process.

Methods for Isolating the Effects of the Program

Decide the technique you plan to use to isolate the effects of the program on your Level 4 measures. The method of isolation is typically the same for all measures, but often you find in working with some measures that you can use one technique, whereas working with other measures may require you to use another technique.

Methods for Converting Data to Monetary Value

Next, determine the methods you will use to convert your Level 4 measures to monetary value. In some cases, you will choose not to convert a measure to monetary value. When that is the case, just leave that space blank. Otherwise, select a technique described in chapter 5.

Cost Categories

This section includes all costs for the program. These costs include the needs assessment, program design and development, program delivery, evaluation costs, and some amount that's representative of the overhead and administrative costs for those people and processes that support your programs. Each cost category is listed on the ROI analysis plan.

Intangible Benefits

Not all measures will be converted to monetary value. There is a four-part test in chapter 5 that helps you decide which measures to convert and which not to convert. Those measures you choose not to convert to monetary value are considered intangible benefits. Move the Level 4 measures that you don't convert to monetary value to this column.

Communication Targets for the Final Report

In many cases, organizations will plan their communication targets in detail. Here, during the evaluation planning phase, you will identify at a minimum those audiences to whom the final report will be submitted. Four key audiences always get a copy or summary of the report: the participants, talent development staff, supervisors of the participants, and client.

Other Influences and Issues During Application

When planning, it's important to anticipate any issues that may occur during the training process that might have a negative effect or no effect on your identified impact measures. You can also use this part of the plan to list any issues you foresee.

Comments

The final element of the ROI analysis plan is the comments. Here, you can put notes to remind yourself and your evaluation team of key issues, comments regarding potential success or failure of the program, reminders for specific tasks to be conducted by the evaluation team, and so forth.

The importance of planning your data collection for your ROI analysis cannot be stressed enough. Planning in detail what you are going to ask, how you are going to ask, who you are going to ask, when you are going to ask, and who will do the asking, along with the key steps in

Chapter 2

Table 2-12. Completed Data Collection Plan

Program: Effective Meetings   Responsibility: _____   Date: _____

Level	Program Objectives	Measures of Success	Data Collection Method	Data Sources	Timing	Responsibilities
1	Reaction and Planned Action					
	• Positive reaction	• Average rating of at least 4.0 on 5.0 scale on quality, usefulness, and achievement of program objectives	• End-of-course questionnaire	• Participants	• End of Course	• Facilitator
	• Planned actions	• 100% submit planned actions	• Completed action plans			
2	Learning					
	• Identify the extent and cost of meetings	• Given cost guidelines, identify the cost of the last three meetings	• Meeting profile	• Participants	• At the beginning of the program (pre)	• Facilitator
	• Identify positives, negatives, and implications of basic meeting issues and dynamics	• From a list of 30 positive and negative meeting behaviors, correctly identify the implications of each behavior	• Written test		• At the end of the program (post)	
	• Acquisition of effective meeting behaviors	• Demonstrate the appropriate response to 8 of 10 active role-play scenarios	• Skill practice observation		• During program	

3	Application and Implementation • Use of effective meeting behaviors • Barriers • Enablers	• Reported change in behavior to planning and conducting meetings • Number and variety of barriers • Number and variety of enablers	• Action plan • Questionnaire (for three groups)	• Participants	• Three months	• Program owner
4	Impact • Time savings from fewer meetings, shorter meetings, and fewer participants (hours savings per month) • Variety of business results measures from more successful meetings	• Time savings • Time savings, cost savings, output improvement, quality improvement, project turnaround, as reported	• Questionnaire (for three groups)	• Participants	• Three months	• Program owner
5	ROI • Target an ROI of at least 25%					

Comments:

Chapter 2

the ROI analysis, will help ensure successful execution. Additionally, having clients sign off on your plans will ensure support when the evaluation results are presented.

Table 2-13 presents a completed ROI analysis plan.

Getting It Done

Now it is time for you to go to work. Before you go any further in this book, select a program that is suitable for ROI. If this is your first ROI study, consider selecting a program in which you are confident that success will be achieved. Success with your first study is an incentive for the next one.

Once you have identified the program, answer the questions presented in Exercise 2-1. In the next chapter, you will learn methods for collecting data and begin developing the data collection plan (Table 2-14).

Exercise 2-1. Questions to Start Thinking About Data Collection

Program:

Evaluation Team:

Expected Date of Completion:

1. What is your purpose in conducting an ROI evaluation on this program?

2. What are the broad program objectives at each level of evaluation?
    Level 1:
    Level 2:
    Level 3:
    Level 4:
    Level 5:

3. What are your measures of success for each objective?
    Level 1:
    Level 2:
    Level 3:
    Level 4:
    Level 5:

4. Transfer your answers to questions 2 and 3 to the first two columns in the data collection plan (Table 2-14).

Table 2-13. Completed ROI Analysis Plan

Program: Effective Meetings _____ Responsibility: _____ Date: _____

Data Items (Usually Level 4)	Methods for Isolating the Effects of the Program	Methods of Converting Data to Monetary Values	Cost Categories	Intangible Benefits	Communication Targets for Final Report	Other Influences or Issues During Application	Comments
• Time savings • Miscellaneous business measures	• Participants' estimates • Participants' estimates	• Hourly wage and benefits • Participants' estimates (using standard values when available)	• Prorated cost of needs assessment • Program fee per participant • Travel, lodging, and meals • Facilities • Participants' salaries plus benefits for time in workshop • Evaluation cost	• Improvement in individual productivity not captured elsewhere • Stress reduction • Improved planning and scheduling • Greater participation in meetings	• Business unit president • Senior managers • Managers of participants • Participants • Training and development staff	• Participants must see the need for providing measurement • Follow-up process will be explained to participants during the program • Three groups will be measured • Participants must report productivity gains due to time saved	Participants will identify specific improvements as a result of meetings being conducted more effectively

Plan Your Work

Chapter 2

Table 2-14. Data Collection Plan

Program: _____ Responsibility: _____ Date: _____

Level	Program Objectives	Measures of Success	Data Collection Method	Data Sources	Timing	Responsibilities
1						
2						
3						
4						
5 ROI						
Comments:						

3

Collect Data

What's Inside This Chapter

This chapter presents the basics in collecting data for your ROI study, which includes:
- selecting the data collection method
- defining the source of data
- determining the time of data collection.

3

Collect Data

Selecting the Method

Evaluation that occurs during program implementation helps show whether the content matters to the target audience. Post-program evaluation gives insight into whether content sticks in such a way that participants apply what they learn, the system supports that application, and impact measures improve.

End-of-Course Data Collection Methods

There are a variety of data collection techniques to assist in gathering the right data from the right source at the right time. The most frequently used data collection approach is the end-of-course questionnaire, which collects Level 1: Reaction and Planned Action data that answers questions related to:

- the program's relevance to the job
- the program's importance to the job
- participant intent to use knowledge and skills learned
- amount of new information offered through the program
- participant willingness to recommend the program to others.

End-of-course questionnaires can also prod participants to think about potential uses of what they have learned in the talent development program as well as the effect these potential uses will have on the organization. Table 3-1 presents a sample end-of-course questionnaire.

Because Level 1 data also include planned actions, an action plan can be used to gather information about specific actions participants intend to take; however, this action plan is not to be confused with that used in collecting follow-up data. Rather, the Level 1 action plan requires participants to list the planned actions and completion dates; there is not necessarily an intent to follow-up. Table 3-2 presents an example.

Table 3-1. End-of-Course Questionnaire

Leading Change in Organizations

Thank you for participating in the Leading Change in Organizations course. This is your opportunity to provide feedback as to how we can improve this course.

Please respond to the following questions regarding your perception of the program as well as your anticipated use of the skills learned during the program. We also would like to know how you think the skills applied from this course will affect business measures important to your function.

You will receive a summary of these results by June 6.

I. Your reaction to the course facilitation	Strongly Disagree 1	2	3	4	Strongly Agree 5
1. The instructor was knowledgeable about the subject.	❑	❑	❑	❑	❑
2. The instructor was prepared for the class.	❑	❑	❑	❑	❑
3. Participants were encouraged to take part in class discussions.	❑	❑	❑	❑	❑
4. The instructor was responsive to participants' questions.	❑	❑	❑	❑	❑
5. The instructor's energy and enthusiasm kept the participants actively engaged.	❑	❑	❑	❑	❑
6. The instructor discussed how I can apply the knowledge and skills taught in the class.	❑	❑	❑	❑	❑
II. Your reaction to the course content	**Strongly Disagree 1**	**2**	**3**	**4**	**Strongly Agree 5**
7. The course content is relevant to my current job.	❑	❑	❑	❑	❑
8. The course content is important to my current job.	❑	❑	❑	❑	❑
9. The material was organized logically.	❑	❑	❑	❑	❑
10. The exercises and examples helped me understand the material.	❑	❑	❑	❑	❑
11. The course content provided new information.	❑	❑	❑	❑	❑
12. I intend to use what I learned in this course.	❑	❑	❑	❑	❑
III. New knowledge and skills acquired in the course	**Strongly Disagree 1**	**2**	**3**	**4**	**Strongly Agree 5**
13. I learned new knowledge and skills from this course.	❑	❑	❑	❑	❑
14. I am confident that I can effectively apply the skills learned in the course.	❑	❑	❑	❑	❑

Table 3-1. End-of-Course Questionnaire (cont.)

IV. Your expected application of knowledge and skills	Strongly Disagree 1	2	3	4	Strongly Agree 5
15. I will effectively apply what I have learned in this course.	❏	❏	❏	❏	❏

16. What percentage of your total work time requires the knowledge and skills presented in this course?
❏ 0% ❏ 10% ❏ 20% ❏ 30% ❏ 40% ❏ 50% ❏ 60% ❏ 70% ❏ 80% ❏ 90% ❏ 100%

17. On a scale of 0% (not at all) to 100% (extremely critical), how critical is applying the content of this course to your job success?
❏ 0% ❏ 10% ❏ 20% ❏ 30% ❏ 40% ❏ 50% ❏ 60% ❏ 70% ❏ 80% ❏ 90% ❏ 100%

18. What percentage of the new knowledge and skills learned from this course do you estimate you will directly apply to your job?
❏ 0% ❏ 10% ❏ 20% ❏ 30% ❏ 40% ❏ 50% ❏ 60% ❏ 70% ❏ 80% ❏ 90% ❏ 100%

19. What potential barriers could prevent you from applying the knowledge and skills learned from this course?

20. What potential enablers will support you in applying the knowledge and skills learned from this course?

IV. How what you learned will impact the business

21. As a result of your applying the knowledge and skills learned in this course, to what extent will the following measures be improved?

	Not at All 1	2	3	4	Completely 5
Productivity	❏	❏	❏	❏	❏
Sales	❏	❏	❏	❏	❏
Quality	❏	❏	❏	❏	❏
Costs	❏	❏	❏	❏	❏
Time	❏	❏	❏	❏	❏
Job Satisfaction	❏	❏	❏	❏	❏
Customer Satisfaction	❏	❏	❏	❏	❏

Table 3-2. Action Plan

Action Plan	
Name: _____	Date: _____
Course: _____	Instructor: _____
Planned Actions	**Completion Date**
1. _____	_____
2. _____	_____
3. _____	_____
4. _____	_____
5. _____	_____

At Level 2, data are collected using a variety of techniques to determine if learning occurred. Fundamental questions answered at Level 2 represent:

- new knowledge and skills acquired
- improvement in knowledge and skills
- confidence to apply knowledge and skills.

While it is sometimes assumed that testing is the only technique to measure knowledge and skill acquisition, there are many other techniques to gather this information. These include:

- written tests and exercises
- criterion reference tests
- performance demonstrations
- performance observations
- case studies
- simulations
- peer assessments
- self-assessments
- skill- and confidence-building exercises.

Technology-enabled learning allows for easier and more integrated data collection at these lower levels of evaluation. By building questions and exercises into a mobile module, for example, participants can respond seamlessly as part of the program. Simple online polling tools are excellent for incorporating data collection into in-person talent development events. By asking questions about the usefulness of content throughout a program and capturing those data in real time, facilitators can address issues and improve programs as they go. Games can also allow for real-time knowledge checks and the opportunity for deeper dive feedback in class.

Integrating data collection during program implementation is relatively easy given the tools available. The real data collection change is in the follow-up when you want to know if people are applying what they learned and how much the impact measures are improving.

Post-Program Data Collection Methods

Post-program data represent those measures of success categorized as Levels 3, 4, and 5. Level 3 follow-up data represent the extent to which participants apply the knowledge and skills learned in the course. Fundamentally, this level of data addresses issues related to participants':

- effectiveness in applying knowledge and skills
- frequency in applying knowledge and skills
- barriers to applying knowledge and skills
- enablers supporting the application of knowledge and skills.

Additionally, Level 3 data may include how much content of a given program participants actually use and how critical that application is to their current job.

Data collected at Level 4 are follow-up data that address the consequence of participants' application of the knowledge and skills. These data serve to report the results of the program in measures of output, quality, cost, time, job satisfaction, customer satisfaction, and work habits and attitudes.

An important step taken at this level of measurement is to isolate program effects on improvements in the impact measures from other influencing factors. More information on this topic is found in chapter 4. At Level 5, monetary value for improvement in impact measures and the cost of the program are collected and compared. Monetary value for improvement in impact measures can be found using standard values, historical costs, internal and external experts, databases, and mathematical modeling, as well as, more subjectively, through the use of estimates from credible sources. Cost data are derived from organization records, supplier records, talent development staff, and participants. Table 3-3 summarizes follow-up data collection techniques.

The most often used methods of data collection for ROI evaluation are questionnaires, interviews, focus groups, action plans, and performance records.

Table 3-3. Follow-Up Data Collection Methods

Method	Level 3	Level 4	Level 5
Survey	✓		
Questionnaire	✓	✓	
Interviews	✓		
Focus groups	✓		
Program assignments	✓		
Action planning	✓	✓	
Performance contracting	✓	✓	
Program follow-up session	✓	✓	
Performance monitoring	✓	✓	
Monetary values			✓
Cost data			✓

Questionnaires

Questionnaires are the most often used data collection technique when conducting an ROI evaluation. Questionnaires are inexpensive and easy to administer. Depending on the length, they take very little of the respondent's time. Questionnaires can be sent via mail, internal mail, and email, or they can be distributed online, either posted on an intranet site or via an electronic survey tool.

Questionnaires also provide versatility in the types of data you can collect. For example, you can gather data about the demographics of participants, attitudes toward the program, knowledge gained during the program, or how the participants applied that knowledge. In the questionnaire, you can ask respondents to tell how much a particular measure is worth. Participants, through a questionnaire, can tell how much a measure has improved. They can also identify other variables that influenced improvements in a given measure, and they can tell the extent of the influence of those variables.

Questions can be open-ended, closed, or forced-choice. Participants may be asked to select multiple responses or one response from an array of options. Likert scale questions are very common in follow-up questionnaires, as are frequency scales, ordinal scales, and paired-comparison scales, along with comparative scales and linear numeric scales. Periodically, you will see an adjective checklist on a questionnaire—just to give the participants the opportunity to reinforce their attitude toward the program.

While questionnaires can be quite lengthy and you can ask any number of questions, the best questionnaires are concise. They reflect those questions that will allow you to gather needed data. However, do not sacrifice thoroughness for brevity; ensure that you cover all the issues necessary to develop the story you want to tell about your program. On the other hand, thoroughness does not mean asking every possible question. Table 3-4 provides a simple questionnaire focused on gathering Level 4 data after the implementation of a coaching program. This brief questionnaire is quite powerful when used to understand the impact of a program and to have participants provide information on both isolating the effects of the initiative and converting data to monetary values.

 Noted

Technology enables us to ask questions in such a way that analysis has never been easier. For example, questions about monetary value can be asked and simply calculated, so that neither the respondents nor the talent development professional has to worry about math. Qualtrics.com is one such tool that provides survey developers and respondents with an improved survey experience.

Interviews

Interviews are the most ideal method of data collection for a deep dive into an issue. They allow you to get more precise data than questionnaires, action plans, and even focus groups. Interviews can be conducted in person or over the phone; online tools like web and video conferencing platforms make participation in the interview process more accessible to hard-to-reach target audiences.

In-person interviews (those done in the same physical room or through virtual platforms) have an advantage over self-administered instruments like questionnaires. One reason is that the person conducting the interview can show the respondent items that can help clarify questions and response options. It also allows the person conducting the interview to observe body language that may indicate that the respondent is uncomfortable with the question, anxious because of time commitments, or not interested in the interview process. Unlike the situation with a paper-based or email questionnaire where the disinterested respondent can simply throw away the questionnaire or press the delete key, in an interview setting, the evaluator can change strategies, in hopes of motivating respondents to participate.

Table 3-4. Sample Data Collection Instrument, Level 4

Coaching Questions

1. To what extent did coaching positively influence the following measures:

	Significant Influence				No Influence	
	5	4	3	2	1	N/A
Productivity	☐	☐	☐	☐	☐	☐
Sales	☐	☐	☐	☐	☐	☐
Quality	☐	☐	☐	☐	☐	☐
Costs	☐	☐	☐	☐	☐	☐
Efficiency	☐	☐	☐	☐	☐	☐
Time	☐	☐	☐	☐	☐	☐
Employee Satisfaction	☐	☐	☐	☐	☐	☐
Customer Satisfaction	☐	☐	☐	☐	☐	☐

2. What other measures were positively influenced by coaching?

3. Of the measures listed above, improvement in which one is most directly linked to coaching? (Check only one)
   ☐ Productivity   ☐ Employee Satisfaction   ☐ Sales   ☐ Quality
   ☐ Cost   ☐ Customer Satisfaction   ☐ Efficiency   ☐ Time

4. Please define the measure above and its unit for measurement

5. How much did the measure identified in Questions 3 and 4 improve since you began this process?
   ☐ Weekly   ☐ Monthly   ☐ Annually

6. What other processes, programs, or events may have contributed to this improvement?

7. Recognizing that other factors may have caused this improvement, estimate the percentage of improvement related directly to coaching?

8. For this measure, what is the monetary value of improvement for one unit of this measure? (Although this is difficult, please make every effort to estimate the value.)

9. Please state your basis for the estimated value of improvement you indicated above.

10. What is the annual value of improvement in the measure you selected above?

11. What confidence do you place in the estimates you have provided in the prior questions? (0 percent is no confidence, 100 percent is complete certainty.)

Interviews are used when the evaluator needs to ask complex questions, or the list of response choices is so long that it becomes confusing if administered through a questionnaire. In-person interviews are conducted when the information collected through the interview process is considered confidential or when the respondent would feel uncomfortable providing the information on paper (or electronically) or over the phone. They also are useful when there is a need to probe for more detail.

Interviews can be structured or unstructured. Structured interviews work exactly like a questionnaire, except that there is a face-to-face rapport between the evaluator and the respondent. The respondent has the opportunity to elaborate on responses, and the evaluator can ask follow-up questions for clarification. Unstructured interviews allow greater depth of dialogue between the evaluator and the respondent.

Virtual interviews using online platforms simulate the in-person interview without the cost of traveling to the same physical room. While some people are less comfortable with this technology, it has many advantages in addition to travel cost avoidance. Virtual face-to-face interviews allow the interviewee and the interviewer to interact as they would in a traditional setting. It let the interviewer to share pictures, websites, and documents that they may not have access to if they were in a physical location other than their office. Virtual platforms also make recording the interview much easier and, in some cases, less threatening to the interviewee. There are few things more uncomfortable than having an audio recorder or mobile device on the table next to you as you're attempting to provide objective responses.

Telephone interviews are also more convenient than traveling to a venue other than the one you are currently in. Some respondents prefer to talk over the telephone, and interview questions can be emailed prior to the telephone call. The disadvantage of telephone interviews is that the personal rapport is not as great as in face-to-face interviews, and the respondent does not have the advantage of the evaluator showing or referring to specific items to clarify issues.

Although interviews provide good data, they can be costly. In planning the data collection, it is important to consider how many interviews you need to hold to gather the appropriate amount of data. In many cases, interviews are conducted only with executives or supervisors of the participants in an effort to supplement participant data. Occasionally, these interviews offer an opportunity to collect new data unavailable from the participants. Also, the purpose of interviewing is to go deep with information gathering, rather than wide, which is the benefit of self-administered instruments like questionnaires. This reduces the number of people to interview.

Scheduling interviews can be a challenge, and getting through the executive's gatekeeper can prove an even a greater challenge than putting the interview on the executive's schedule once you do make it through. If possible, depending on the cost of the program and how much you want to spend on the evaluation, you might consider hiring a professional interviewer. At the very least, it is recommended that you take a course or training in interviewing skills. The interviewing process can be quite daunting if you are uncomfortable with the questions being asked, such as those questions with regard to Level 4 measures, isolation, and data conversion.

Also, if you are evaluating a program offered inside your organization, your likely target for the interview is someone else working within the organization. This may be intimidating to the interviewee, deterring them from presenting the most objective data. It may also be intimidating to you, preventing you from asking the right questions or drilling down into detail when you need to. A third-party interviewer can often remove that intimidation factor.

Focus Groups

Focus groups are a good way to get important information from a group of people when dialogue among the group is important. Focus groups work best when the topic on which participants are to focus is important to them. High-quality focus groups and the questions you ask produce discussions that address exactly the topics you want to hear about. The key to successful focus groups, however, is keeping the focus group on topic. While focus groups are used for group discussion, a fair amount of planning goes into designing the protocol. The conversations that transpire during the focus group are constructed conversations focusing on a key issue of interest. Table 3-5 presents a sample focus group protocol used to collect Level 3 data for a study of an emergency response support program.

Noted

Collecting data using qualitative techniques such as interviews and focus groups is a noble idea, but one that often falls short of its real potential. Two challenges present themselves. The first challenge is transcribing interview and focus group responses. The second is making meaning out of the data. Gig workers, machine learning, and artificial intelligence (AI) are enabling researchers to tackle both issues with more ease than in the past, enabling evaluators to leverage the value qualitative data have to offer.

Table 3-5. Focus Group Protocol for a Study of an Emergency Response Support Program

Focus Group Facilitator Protocol

Purpose

This focus group is intended to help us understand how knowledge and skills gained in the program have been applied (Level 3). During the focus group you will identify effectiveness with application, frequency of application, barriers, and enablers to application.

What to Do

1. Give yourself extra time.
2. Arrive a few minutes early to prepare the room.
3. Introduce yourself to the point of contact. Reinforce the purpose and explain the process.
4. Set up the room so that the tables or chairs are in a U-shape so participants can see each other, and you can become part of the group.
5. Place tent cards at each seat.
6. As participants arrive, introduce yourself, give them refreshments, and chat a few minutes.
7. As you ask questions, your partner should write the answers, but not try to write every word. Listen for key issues and quotes that are meaningful, make important points, and reinforce use of knowledge and skills.
8. When you have gathered the information you need, thank each person. Clean up, thank your point of contact, and leave.
9. Find a place to debrief with your partner and clarify notes. Do it immediately, because you will surely forget something.
10. When you return to your workplace, analyze the data.

What to Take

1. Directions.
2. Point of contact's telephone numbers.
3. Tent cards. Each tent card should have a number in a corner. Participants can write their first name just so you call them by name, but your notes will refer to the participant number.
4. Refreshments—something light, but a treat because people respond to food, and it relaxes the environment.
5. Flipchart.
6. Markers for the tent cards and the flipchart.
7. Focus group notepads.
8. An umbrella.

What to Wear

You will be in a comfortable environment, so ties and high-heels are not necessary, but do dress professionally. No jeans and tennis shoes: business casual.

What to Say

The intent is to understand how participants are applying what they learned during training. Start on time. You do not want to keep the participants over the allotted time.

1. Thank everyone for participating.
2. Introduce yourself and your partner. Tell them you are part of a research team conducting a study on the program. Reinforce with them that their input is important to this study. The results of the study will be used to improve training and other program support initiatives.
3. Share the purpose of the focus group.
4. Explain how the process will work and that their input is strictly confidential.
5. Have them put their first name on the tent card. Explain that the numbers in the corner of the tent card are for recording purposes and that in no way will their name be recorded. Explain that after the focus group you and your partner will compile notes; your notes will be later compiled with those of the other focus groups. Also, tell them that their input in the focus group is supplemental to a questionnaire that they may have already received.
6. Begin Question 1 with Participant 1.

Questions

Each person will answer each question before moving to the next question. The idea is to allow each person to hear what the others say so that they can reflect on their responses. You want to know what each individual thinks.

1. Now that you have had a chance to apply what you learned regarding your emergency response duties, how effectively have you been able to execute those duties?
2. What specific barriers have interfered with your ability to execute your duties?
3. What has supported your efforts?

Focus Group Note Pad

Question:

Notes	Notable Quotes

Date: _____

Location: _____

Facilitator: _____

Page ___ of ___

Chapter 3

Action Plans

In some cases, action plans are incorporated into the talent development program, with participants completing one prior to leaving the program. Action plans are used to collect Level 3: Application and Implementation and Level 4: Impact data. They can also be used to collect monetary values of measures and isolate program effects when more robust approaches are inappropriate.

Action plans are completed during the program. The results, categorized as Level 1: Reaction and Planned Action, give participants a road map toward implementation of content. Sometime after the program, the action plans will be reviewed to determine if actions actually occurred, resulting in Level 3: Application and Implementation data. Using action plans as a tool to collect Level 4: Impact data, however, takes more effort.

Table 3-6 shows an action plan used to collect Levels 3 and 4 data. In Section A, the participants include their name, objective, evaluation period, measure for improvement, current performance, and target performance. Identifying these measures prior to the program is an important step in securing credible follow-up data. During the program, participants complete Sections B and C with specific steps they will take, the end results of those steps, and expected intangible benefits. Questions 1, 2, and 3 in Section E are completed prior to the participant coming to the program.

After the evaluation period ends, participants complete Questions 4, 5, 6, and 7 in Section E. In answering Question 4, the participant indicates how much that measure actually changed during the last month of the evaluation period compared to the average before the training. The participant also explains the basis for this change. It is important that all claims of improvement and monetary benefit are supported to ensure the credibility of any estimate participants provide. Questions 5, 6, and 7 are then completed. These questions represent participant perception of the

Basic Rule 3

Extreme data items and unsupported claims should not be used in ROI calculations.

contribution the program had on improvement in the measures. While not the ideal approach to isolate program effects, it leads to a more credible story than does giving the program full credit for the improvement. (See chapter 4 for more information on isolating the effects of programs.) Section F provides information about actual intangible benefits, which round-out the story, giving stakeholders a view of success from multiple perspectives including quantitative, qualitative, financial, and nonfinancial data.

Table 3-6. Sample Action Plan for Levels 3 and 4 Data

Part I. Action Plan for the Leadership 101 Training Program   SAMPLE

A

Name: Medicine Gelatin Manager   **Instructor Signature:** _____   **Follow-Up Date:** _____

Objective: Elimination of Gel Waste   **Evaluation Period:** June 1 to November 30

Improvement Measure: Quality   **Current Performance:** 8,000 kg wasted monthly   **Target Performance:** Reduce waste by 80 percent

B

Specific Steps: I will do this	End Result: So that
1. Take a more active role in daily gelatin schedule to ensure the manufacture and processing control of gelatin quantities. 2. Inform supervisors and technicians on the value of gelatin and make them aware of waste. 3. Be proactive to gelatin issues before they become a problem. 4. Constantly monitor hours of encapsulation lines on all shifts to reduce downtime and eliminate the possibility of leftover batches. 5. Provide constant feedback to all in the department including encaps machine operators.	1. Better control of gelatin production on a daily basis. This will eliminate the making of excess gelatin that could be waste. 2. Charts and graphs with dollar values of waste will be provided to give awareness and a better understanding of the true value of waste. 3. Make gelatin for encapsulation lines and making better decisions on the amounts. 4. Eliminate the excess manufacturing of gelatin mass and the probability of leftover medicine batches. 5. Elimination of unnecessary gelatin mass waste.

Expected Intangible Benefits

C

Gel mass will decrease to a minimum over time, which will contribute to great financial gains for our company (material variance) and put dollars into the bottom line.

Chapter 3

Table 3-6. Sample Action Plan for Levels 3 and 4 Data (cont.)

Part II. Action Plan for the __Leadership 101__ Training Program   SAMPLE

D

Name: Medicine Gelatin Manager   **Objective:** Elimination of Gel Waste

Improvement Measure: Quality   **Current Performance:** 8,000 kg wasted monthly   **Target Performance:** Reduce waste by 80 percent

Analysis

E

1. What is the unit of measure? __Waste reduction__   Does this measure reflect your performance alone?   Yes ☐   No ☑
   If not, how many employees are represented in the measure? __32__

2. What is the value (cost) of one unit? __$3.60 per kilogram of gelatin mass.__

3. How did you arrive at this value? __This is the cost of raw materials and is the value we use for waste.__

4. How much did this measure change during the last month of the evaluation period compared to the average before the training program? (monthly value) __2,000 kg monthly waste.__

5. Please explain the basis of this change and what you or your team did to cause it. __6,000 kilograms of waste eliminated. Reduction in machines from 19 to 12 created additional savings, but did not calculate. Gains in machine hours (efficiency) in the encaps dept. More awareness of gel mass waste and its costs. Key contributing factors were problem solving skills, communicating with my supervisors and technicians and their willing response, as well as my ability to manage the results.__

6. What level of confidence do you place on the above information? (100% = certainty | 0% = no confidence) __70%__

7. What percentage of this change was actually caused by the application of the skills from the __Leadership 101__ training program (0–100%) __20%__

8. If your measure is time savings, what percentage of the time saved was actually applied toward productive tasks? (0–100%) __N/A__

Actual Intangible Benefits

F

Gelatin mass waste has been a problem for our company since startup; with low efficiency in the encapsulation department and the mistakes made in the gel department, the waste was out of control. In the past few months efficiency has increased and the gel department has stabilized. As a result, waste is down considerably.

The action planning process should be an integral part of the talent development program, not an add-on or optional activity. To gain the maximum effectiveness from the use of action plans, the following steps should be considered:

Basic Rule 4

Estimates of improvements should be adjusted for the potential error of the estimate.

- **Communicate the action plan requirement early in the talent development process.** The most negative reaction to the action planning process comes when it is a surprise to participants. Prior to coming to the program, participants need to be aware of the expectations and that the action planning process is part of it. When participants realize the benefits of the action planning process and that the program is intended to improve key impact measures, they will take the program and the process more seriously.
- **Describe the action planning process at the beginning of the program.** While the action planning process is presented prior to participants attending the talent development program, it is important to reintroduce the action plan at the beginning of the first day of the program. This keeps the participants focused on the need to complete the action plan, as well as on the impact measures they are intended to improve, while they participate in the program.
- **Teach the action planning process.** An important prerequisite for action plan success is to understand how it works. Part of the program's agenda should be allocated to this process.
- **Allow time to develop the plan.** If the action planning process is an integrated part of the program, time should be included during the course period to complete the action plan.
- **Have the facilitator approve the action plan.** The action plan must be related to the program objectives and represent an important accomplishment for the organization when it is completed. It is helpful to have the facilitator fully engaged in the process and sign off on the action plan, ensuring that it reflects all the requirements and is appropriate for the specific program. In some cases, a space is provided for the facilitator's signature on the action plan.
- **Require participants to assign monetary value for improvement.** This step allows participants the opportunity to contribute to the data conversion step that helps move the evaluation to Level 5: ROI. For this step to be effective, it may be helpful to provide examples of typical ways in which values can be assigned to actual data.

- **Ask participants to isolate the effects of the program.** Although the action plan itself is an influence on improvement in impact measures, other factors will also influence that improvement. While completing the action plan during the follow-up, participants should estimate the improvement of their Level 4 measures that are related to the program.
- **Ask participants to provide confidence levels for estimates.** While some talent development professionals push back on this step, its purpose is to ensure the most conservative estimate is given. It also offers some level of reliability that allows for comparison between results of different program evaluations.
- **Require action plans to be presented to the group.** Have participants present their action plans to help ensure that the process is thoroughly developed and encourages implementing actions on the job.
- **Explain the follow-up mechanisms.** Participants should leave the talent development program with a clear understanding of how the action plans will be followed. Some options for the follow-up process are:
    o Have the group reconvene to discuss progress on the plans.
    o Have participants meet with their immediate managers and discuss the success of the plan.
    o Have the program evaluator, the participant, and the immediate manager meet to discuss the plans and any information contained in it.
    o Have participants send the plans to the evaluator and discuss it with them on a conference call.
    o Have participants send the plans directly to the talent development department with no meetings or discussions.
- **Collect action plans at the predetermined follow-up time.** Because the action planning process is built into the program, action plan response rates are typically very high.
- **Summarize the data and calculate the ROI.** Once all the action plans have been submitted, the data derived from the action plans, including the monetary benefits for the measures improved, get incorporated into the ROI equation.

While the action plan process is beneficial, there are disadvantages. For example, participants have no assurance of anonymity for information they provide. The action planning process can also be somewhat time consuming for the participant and the supervisor. However, if both believe the program is important and that it is intended to improve critical measures in their work unit, the action planning process will be supported and can prove to be a valuable tool.

Performance Records

Performance records are records of standard data important throughout the organization in reporting performance status for a variety of functions. It would be a wise investment of your time to learn what data are currently housed within your organization, who has access to the data, and how you can best access the data if you need to. You may find there is more available than you think.

Response Rates

An often-asked question when considering the data that are collection process is, "How many responses do you need in order for the data to be valid and usable?" The typical approach to determining the response rate needed for an accurate story of success and valid evaluation results is to first consider the population and how diverse or homogeneous the population is in terms of factors that could influence their responses. The next consideration is how confident you want to be that the sample responds the same as the population would given a certain margin of error. Based on these considerations, you would target a sample that was smaller than the population, and, with the results, infer the findings to the larger population. While sampling has more technical components than a simple calculator provides, you can get a good rough estimate of an appropriate sample size by using the various online calculators available to you.

The thing to the remember is that a population is made up of people who know the answers to the questions you ask. When evaluating a program, the population includes people who have been through it; the population is not the target audience. Typically, when conducting an ROI study, the population is a small group and results are reported for that group. While others may have completed the program, capturing enough data to make a statistically significant inference based on the study group is often not feasible. The more people involved in an evaluation, the more the evaluation will cost. So, the results of the program evaluation focus on the study group. Then, logical inference, versus statistical inference, comes into play when answering the question, "How likely do the results reflect the results of the entire group?"

Another issue to consider that can affect the results of the study group is the response rate from that group. Without enough responses from your small study group, you could face a problem making assumptions for that group. Let's say you have a program you plan to implement and evaluate that will include a population of 50 people. Based on a sample size calculation, you would

> **Think About This**
>
> Collecting the right data at the right time from the right people is critical to the assessment and evaluation of talent development programs. We asked Trish Uhl, founder of Talent Learning Analytics Leadership Forum and recognized leader in the digitization of learning measurement, a question: How is digital transformation influencing what data we collect, how we collect it, and from whom we collect it?
>
> Here is what she told us:
>
> Organizations are on a digital transformation journey, which is shifting traditional business economics from valuing tangible things to valuing information flows as business assets. In fact, many organizations are building proprietary data science platforms that integrate historical operational data, real-time operational data, big data, and extant data into artificial intelligence and analytics-driven technology ecosystems. These are engineered to explore the combined data to discover actionable insights that can be operationalized for competitive advantage.
>
> For learning and talent development to be part of this flow, we must radically change how we consider, collect, and analyze data. This will require us to dramatically reposition ourselves, our products, our programs, and our data within the larger organizational context. We can no longer operate in a linear value chain where our output (products, programs, data) is divorced from the rest of the business. Instead, we should draw from and contribute to the larger organizational data exchange and ecosystem. In this ecosystem of cross-functional departments, customers, and suppliers, talent development provides value by exchanging data, sharing data, and making data available, as well as using it to discover, deliver, and take action on analytically driven insights that promote organizational agility and competitive differentiation. To be effective, our solutions should be engineered with an eye toward delivering and capturing data. Our product and program design must leverage broader enterprise data and embed bidirectional feedback loops that add and analyze data from the ecosystem.
>
> Consider digital learning technologies, such as intelligent agents or chatbots. We can create a chatbot to provide post-training performance support, and it can be trained to provide that support using insights from enterprise ecosystem data. We can also add the data from conversations with the chatbot to the enterprise ecosystem and gain further analysis from that. Dynamic connections can then be made to evaluate outcomes—to determine whether the solution is hitting the mark. If it's not, we can optimize, redeploy, and reassess, continuously improving the program until we achieve the desired results.
>
> Talent development professionals must commit to our own digital transformation. We can only raise our awareness of the organization's broader digital strategy by becoming digitally fluent ourselves. Only then can we have clarity and understanding of how our products, programs, data, and platforms coexist within the enterprise ecosystem, positioning us as meaningful contributors to the people and organizations we serve.

need responses from 48 people to ensure a 95 percent level of confidence and a 5 percent margin of error, which tend to be conventional targets. It is possible that your response rate will be lower. So, making inference with any level of confidence to nonrespondents becomes more challenging. To address the issue, the ROI Methodology follows a simple standard, Guiding Principle #6 (from chapter 2): If no improvement data are available for a population or from a specific source, assume that little or no improvement has occurred. Applying this principle means that for those people who do not provide data, you will make no judgment with regard to their performance or to the impact the program made on business measures that they may have observed. Using this guiding principle as the standard, you are eliminating the issue of inferring to the larger population, being conservative in your reporting, and positioning your evaluation results so that they can be compared to the results of similar studies. But, given this principle, it is important that you receive as many responses as possible from the people involved in the evaluation.

Table 3-7 lists a variety of action items that can be taken to ensure an appropriate response rate. It all starts with providing advanced communication about the evaluation. No one likes to be hit with a detailed questionnaire unannounced. First, it only adds to participants' daily tasks, and second, some of the questions can be quite challenging if a heads-up has not been given. Clearly communicate the reason for the evaluation and for the questionnaire. Participants need to understand that the evaluation is not about them, it is about improving the program. Identify those people who will see the results of the evaluation and assure them that they will get a summary of the evaluation. Keep the questionnaire as brief as possible. Ask only those questions that are important to the evaluation. If you can afford it, have a third party collect and analyze the data so that participants feel comfortable that their responses will be held in confidence.

Think About This

Consider how you would manage the administration of a detailed, follow-up questionnaire. The following is a data collection administration plan with three sections. The first section represents actions you can take prior to the distribution of the questionnaire. The second section represents actions you can take during the evaluation process. The third section represents actions you can take after the evaluation process. Think about the things you can do that will help ensure you get a successful response rate to your data collection efforts and add them to the list.

Before the evaluation begins, we will:
✓ Ask our senior executive to submit a letter announcing the importance of the evaluation.
✓ _____

During the evaluation, we will:
✓ Send a reminder one week after the questionnaire is administered.
✓ _____

After the evaluation is complete, we will:
✓ Send all respondents a summary copy of the results.
✓ _____

Table 3-7. Actions to Improve Response Rates for Questionnaires

Increasing Questionnaire Response Rates

- Provide advance communication about the questionnaire.
- Clearly communicate the reason for the questionnaire.
- Indicate who will see the results of the questionnaire.
- Show how the data will be integrated with other data.
- Let participants know what actions will be taken based on the data.
- Keep the questionnaire simple and brief.
- Allow for responses to be anonymous—or at least confidential.
- Make it easy to respond; include a self-addressed, stamped envelope or return email address.
- If appropriate, let the target audience know that they are part of a carefully selected sample.
- Provide one or two follow-up reminders using a different medium.
- Get the introduction letter signed by a top executive or administrator.
- Enclose a giveaway item with the questionnaire (pen, money, and so forth).
- Provide an incentive (or chance of incentive) for quick response.
- Send a summary of results to target audience.
- Distribute the questionnaire to a captive audience.
- Consider an alternative distribution channel, such as email.
- Have a third party collect and analyze the data.
- Communicate the time limit for submitting responses.
- Review the questionnaire at the end of the formal session.
- Allow for completion of the survey during normal work hours.
- Add emotional appeal.
- Design the questionnaire to attract attention using a professional format.
- Provide options to respond (paper, email, website).
- Use a local coordinator to help distribute and collect questionnaires.
- Frame questions so participants can respond appropriately and accurately.

Source: Phillips and Phillips (2016)

Considerations When Selecting a Method

A first consideration when selecting a data collection method is the culture of the organization. How have other types of data collection been conducted in the past? Some organizations are averse to questionnaires. If this is the case, you may struggle with getting questionnaires back for your evaluation. Some organizations support data collection via questionnaire as along as it is automated. Consider the culture and use the method that best fits.

Along with organizational culture, there are additional issues that should be considered when selecting the data collection method, such as validity and reliability, time and cost, and utility.

Validity and Reliability

When selecting a data collection method, consider the technique that will give the most valid and reliable results. Keep in mind that you will have to balance accuracy with the cost of data collection. Only spend 5 to 10 percent of the fully loaded cost of the program on the ROI study. Evaluation should not cost more than the program itself. Because all evaluation costs are included in the denominator of the ROI formula, this further drives down the ROI percentage. But, you do want to use the technique that will provide the best data.

 Think About This

In a study of a state-level capacity-building program, the evaluators were asked to design a questionnaire to see if program volunteers believed that it was achieving its intended objectives. The evaluators asked the corporate office that was funding this program to sample a small number of participants to ensure the questions were measuring what was intended to be measured and that participants understood questions being asked. Rather than count on the participants to test the questionnaire, the corporate office ran the questionnaire up the ladder; all managers tied to the program said, "Yes, the questions represented the correct measures." However, when the questionnaire was distributed to the volunteers, the volunteers indicated that in no way did the questions represent what the program was intended to do.

Take care when developing your questionnaires to ensure that participants realize the intent of the program and that subject matter experts realize the actual application of the program.

A basic way to look at validity is to ask yourself, "Are you measuring what you intend to measure?" While validity assessment can be determined using sophisticated modeling approaches, the most basic approach is using your subject matter experts and participants, along with additional resources such as literature reviews and previous case studies. Do your questions match the other questions asked when measuring the same type of program? Do your subject matter experts agree that the measures being taken represent the intended objectives of the program? Meanwhile, face validity means answering the question, "Do the questions make sense to the participants?" A simple sampling of potential participants to review the questionnaire can provide some indication that the questions are feasible.

While validity is concerned with whether you are measuring the right measures, reliability is concerned with whether respondents are consistent in their answers. The most basic test of reliability is repeatability. This is the ability to get the same data from several measurements made in the same way. A basic example of repeatability is administering the questionnaire to the same person repeatedly over a period of time. If the person responds the same way to the questions every time, there is minimum error, meaning there is high reliability. If, however, the participant randomly selected the answers, there would be high error, meaning there is low reliability.

Time and Cost

When selecting data collection methods, several issues should be considered with regard to time and cost. Consider the time required for participants to complete the instrument. Also, consider the time required for participants' supervisors to complete the instrument or coach the participants through the data collection process. Remember, everything spent on data collection, including time for the completion of data collection instruments, is a cost to the program. Consider the overall cost of data collection, which includes printing costs and time to develop and test the questionnaire or whatever data collection instrument you plan to use. Consider the amount of disruption that the data collection will cause employees. Typically interviews and focus groups require the greatest disruption, however, they also provide the best data. Balance the accuracy of the data you need to make a decision about the program with what it will cost you to gather the data.

Utility

The last consideration when selecting a data collection method is utility. How useful will the data be, given the type of data you'll be collecting through the data collection process? Data collected through a questionnaire can be easily coded and put into a database and analyzed. With the help of automation, data generated through a questionnaire can quickly be summarized and the story of success be told. Data collected through focus groups and interviews, however, call for a more challenging approach to analysis. Though you often take those stories collected through dialogue with your respondents and summarize the story in your report, a better analysis of what your respondents are telling you can be conducted. This requires developing themes for the data collected and coding those themes for statistical analysis. This type of analysis can be quite time consuming and, in some cases, frustrating if you do not immediately compile the data at the conclusion of the interview or focus group. Although you often make mental notes during data collection of this type, you will quickly lose those notes if you don't record them in some structured way.

Another issue with regard to utility is, what can you do with the data? If the question does not map back to an objective of the program, reconsider asking it. Also, whether the programs are being offered through a corporate, government, nonprofit, community, or faith-based setting, the results will influence a business decision of some kind. If you can't use the data for this purpose, don't ask the question.

Defining the Source

Selecting the source of the data is critical in ensuring data accuracy. Sometimes it is necessary to go to multiple sources of data. A fundamental question should be answered when deciding on the source: Who (or what system) knows best about the measures you are taking?

The primary source of data is the participants. No one knows more about their perception of a program, what they learned, and how they are applying what they learned than the participants themselves. Participants are also a good source for Level 4 data, monetary values, and isolating techniques. Typical sources for Levels 3, 4, and 5 include performance records, participants, participants' supervisors and managers, participants' peers and direct reports, senior managers and executives, and customers.

Performance Records

Given the variety of sources for the data, one of the most credible will be your organization or internal performance records. These records are not an individual's performance record kept between the individual, the supervisor, and HR. Rather they reflect performance in a work unit, department, division, region, or organization. Performance records can include all types of measures that are usually readily available throughout the organization. This is the preferred method of data collection for Level 4 evaluation, because it usually reflects business impact data.

Participants

Participants are the primary and most widely used source of data for ROI analysis. They are always asked about their reaction to the program, and they are whom you assess to determine if learning has occurred. They know what they do with what they learned when they return to the job, as well as what may prevent them from applying what they learned on the job. In addition, they are the ones who realize what impact their actions have on the job.

Although many people perceive participants as the most biased option, you have to keep in mind that people are typically honest. If you explain and reinforce to the participants that the evaluation is not about them, it is about the program, they will more likely remove their personal feelings from their answers and provide more objective data than if they are uncertain of your intent.

Participants' Supervisors and Managers

Supervisors and managers of the participants are another important source. In many situations, they will observe the participants as they attempt to use the knowledge and skills. Those managers, who are actively engaged in a learning process, will often serve as coaches to ensure that application of newly acquired knowledge and insights occurs. In gathering data from the supervisors, there still remains potential bias.

Participants' Peers and Direct Reports

In evaluating at Level 3, participants' peers and direct reports are good sources of data, especially when you are implementing 360-degree feedback evaluation. Although gathering their input can increase the cost of the evaluation, their perspective may add a level of objectivity to the process.

Senior Managers and Executives

Senior managers and executives also provide valuable data, especially when you are collecting Level 4 data. Their input, however, is somewhat limited because they are removed from the actual application of the knowledge and skills. Senior managers and executives are good sources of data when implementing programs such as a high-profile, expensive leadership development program or other major initiatives in which they are directly involved.

Customers

If measures for improvement are customer related, the customer is the best source of data. A simple example is if you want to know whether the cashier acknowledged the customer in a friendly tone when the customer walked up to check out; the credit card reader can pose a question to the customer who, at the point of sale, can respond. Or, if you want to know whether the customer's perception of customer service has improved, you can send a survey or text and have them respond. Customer data are routinely collected and in a variety of ways; the customer's voice is the ultimate voice you want to hear when determining the direction of your business. But from a training evaluation perspective, the customer's voice is not easily accessible. So, you may need to rely on other sources to provide input from the customer.

Other Sources

Internal and external expert and external databases provide a good source of data for some measures. Experts such as the business intelligence unit or the human capital analytics team can offer insights into improvement in measures that you may not have available. Experts and databases can also be resources for the monetary value of measures when you need it. The key to success in selecting sources of data, as mentioned previously, is to consider who knows best about the measures being taken? And from whom can you get the data most easily?

Determining the Time of Data Collection

The last consideration in the data collection process is the timing of data collection. Typically, Level 3 data collection occurs no longer than three months after the program, depending on the program. Some programs, in which skills should be applied immediately upon conclusion of the program, should be measured earlier—anywhere from 30 days to two months after the program. Sometimes Level 3 data are collected at multiple points in time, particularly when the Level 4: Impact data will be collected beyond the three-month mark.

While the ROI calculation considers the annual benefit of a program, it is atypical to wait an entire year to determine if improvement has occurred in a measure. Senior executives won't wait; the problem will either go away, executives and senior managers will forget, or a decision will be made without the data. Collect the Level 4 measures either at the time of Level 3 data collection or soon after when impact has occurred. Then, annualize the improvement in the measure, convert it to monetary benefits, and include the value in the ROI calculation.

Determining the timing of data collection for follow-up data can be tricky, so it is important to make the timing decision when establishing the program objectives. When deciding on the timing, consider the current state with the measure, the time it will take for participants to use what they learn on a routine basis, the availability of the data, and the convenience and constraints of collecting it.

Getting It Done

In the previous chapter, you read about developing objectives and you worked through the process of defining the measures of your program. Now it is time to complete the data collection plan. Complete the data collection plan from chapter 2 (Table 2-15) by noting which data collection method you plan to use to collect your data at the various levels, the sources of your data, the timing for your data collection, and the person or team responsible for the data collection.

In the next chapter, you will learn to make your results credible by isolating the effects of the program from other influences that may have contributed to business impact.

4

Isolate Program Impact

What's Inside This Chapter

This step in the ROI Methodology attempts to delineate the direct contribution caused by the talent development program, isolating it from other influences. This chapter covers three critical areas:

- understanding why isolating impact is a key issue
- identifying the methods to do it
- building credibility with the process.

4

Isolate Program Impact

Understanding Why Isolating Impact Is a Key Issue

Isolating the effects of a program on business impact data is one of the most challenging yet necessary steps in the ROI Methodology. When addressed credibly, this step links learning directly to improvement in key performance measures.

Other Factors Always Exist

In almost every situation, multiple factors influence organizational performance. The world does not stand still as employees participate in a talent development program. Many functions in the organization are attempting to improve the same metrics as the talent development function. A situation where no other factors enter into the process would be rare. Important arguments exist that support the need to take this step.

Without Isolating Impact, There Is No Alignment—Evidence Versus Proof

Without taking steps to show the contribution, the alignment between programs and improvement in organizational measures does not exist. There may be evidence that a program might make a difference, but there is no accounting for what other factors may have contributed to the improvement. Proving the connection between programs and performance improvement is what this step in the process is all about—isolating the effects of the program.

Other Factors and Influences Have Protective Owners

The owners of the other processes influencing results are convinced that their processes made the difference. When sales increase, marketing and advertising each believe their efforts are the cause and they present a compelling case to management, stressing their achievements. The IT department also believes that technology made the difference. They, likewise, can present a compelling case. In real situations, other processes, such as performance improvement, reward systems, and job redesign, have protective owners, and those owners often can be very convincing that they made a difference.

The challenge of isolating the effects of the program on impact data is critical and can be done; however, it is not easy for very complex programs, especially when strong-willed owners of other processes are involved. It takes a determination to address this situation every time an ROI study is conducted. Fortunately, a variety of approaches is available.

Think About This

You have conducted a sales training program to improve sales competencies for client relationship managers. This program is designed to increase sales as the managers use the competencies. Three months after the training, sales have increased. However, during the evaluation period, product marketing and promotion increased. Also, prices were lowered in two key product lines and new technologies enabled the sales representatives to secure quotes faster, thus increasing efficiency and boosting sales. All these factors influence sales. From the perspective of the sales training function, the challenge is to determine how much of the sales increase is due to the training. If a method is not implemented to show the contribution and talent development claims full credit for improvement in measures, the talent development staff will lose credibility.

Without Isolating Impact, the Study Is Not Valid

Without addressing this issue, your evaluation study is not valid because there are almost always other factors in the mix and the direct connection to learning is not apparent.

Above all, without first isolating the impact, there are two things that you should not do:
1. Take all the credit for the improvement without tackling the issue.
2. Do nothing, attempting to ignore the issue altogether.

Neither of these help the talent development team connect their efforts to the business.

Myths About Isolating the Effects of the Program

Several myths about isolating the effects of the program permeate talent development functions and create concerns, confusion, and frustration with this process. Some researchers, talent development professionals, and consultants inflame this matter by suggesting that isolating the effects is not necessary. Here are the most common myths:

- **Talent development is complementary with other processes; therefore, you should not attempt to isolate its effects on performance improvement.** True, talent development programs are complementary to other factors, all of which drive results. But if a project sponsor needs to understand the relative contribution of talent development, you must tackle isolating the impact. If accomplished properly, it will show how all the complementary factors are working together to drive the improvements.

- **Other functions in the organization do not isolate the effects.** While some functions do not grapple with this issue because they try to make a convincing case that the improvement is related to their own processes, others do isolate their effects. You need a credible approach to address this issue. Notice the next time you complete a customer survey after you make a purchase or open a new account—do they ask you why you made the purchase? They are trying to isolate the results of multiple variables.

- **If you cannot use a comparison group analysis (a research-based control group), then you should not attempt this step.** Although a comparison group analysis is the most credible approach, using one is not feasible in all situations. Consequently, other methods must be used to isolate the effects. The problem does not go away just because you cannot use your desired or favorite method. The challenge is to find other methods that are effective and will work anytime, even if they are not as credible as the comparison group method.

- **The stakeholders will instinctively understand the linkage; therefore, you do not need to attempt to isolate the effects of learning on impact measures.** Unfortunately, stakeholders see and understand what is presented to them. If they do not see the linkage, it is likely they will assume there is none. In fact, in 2009, ATD and the ROI Institute conducted a study to determine what CEOs thought about their investment in talent development. Of the findings, one was that 74 percent of CEOs wanted to see a direct connection between talent development and improvement in impact measures, yet only 4 percent were seeing it (Phillips and Phillips 2009). Another study by Harvard Business Review Analytic Services (2017) reported that only 24 percent of C-suite executives are provided data that connect people metrics to business metrics. Without the proper information, stakeholders will struggle to understand the linkage, particularly when others are claiming full credit for the improvement.

- **Estimates of improvement provide no value.** The last-resort scenario is to tackle isolating the impact by using estimates from the individuals who understand the process the most. Although this should be your last choice, it may provide value and be a credible process, particularly when the estimates are adjusted for the error of the estimate. Estimates are used routinely in other functions.

- **Ignore the issue; maybe they won't think about it.** Unfortunately, audiences are becoming more sophisticated regarding isolating impact, and they are aware of multiple influences. If no attempt is made to isolate the effects of learning, the audience will assume that the other factors have had a tremendous effect, and maybe all the effect. Thus, credibility deteriorates.

These myths underscore the tremendous importance of addressing this issue. If you do not tackle this issue, others will—leaving talent development with less than their desired budgets, resources, and respect. This is not to suggest that talent development does not work in harmony with other processes. All groups should be working together to move organizations in the right direction. However, when funding is provided to different functions in the organization—with different process owners—there is always a struggle to show, and sometimes even to understand, the connection between what they do and the results.

Applying the Techniques

Before the specific techniques are discussed, it is helpful to review two important principles. First, the chain of impact should be revisited. Although the isolation step can be conducted on Level 3: Application and Implementation data (separating the influence of other factors on the actual behavioral change), it is usually applied to Level 4: Impact data. This is the level where the concerns are most frequently raised. The amount of impact connected to the program is a key issue. After the impact data have been collected, the next step in the analysis is to isolate the effects of the program. This is the proof that talent development made a difference.

Second, there needs to be an attempt to identify the other factors that have contributed to the improvement in the business results measures. This step recognizes that other factors are almost always present and that the credit for improvement is shared with other functions in the organization. Just taking this step is likely to gain respect from the management team.

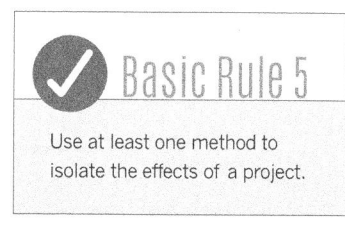

Basic Rule 5

Use at least one method to isolate the effects of a project.

Several potential sources can help identify these influencing factors. The sponsors of the project may be able to identify the factors. Subject matter experts, process owners, and those

Chapter 4

who are most familiar with the situation may be able to indicate what has changed to influence the results. In many situations, participants know what other factors have influenced their performance. After all, it is their direct performance that is being measured and monitored.

By taking stock of this issue, all factors that contributed to improvement are revealed, indicating the seriousness of the issue and underscoring how difficult it is going to be to isolate the effects of the program.

The following are four techniques most frequently used to isolate the effects of talent development programs: control group arrangement, trend line analysis, mathematical modeling, and expert estimation.

Control Group Arrangement

The most accurate and credible approach to isolating the effects of talent development programs is control group arrangement or experimental design. This approach involves the use of an experimental group that attends the program and a control group that does not. The composition of both groups should be as similar as possible, and, if feasible, the selection of participants for each group should be on a random basis. When this is possible and both groups are subjected to the same environmental influences, the differences in the performance of the two groups can be attributed to the training program.

There are different approaches to experimental design. One is the classic design where pre-program measures are collected prior to the program and then the change in performance for each group is compared. There is also post-program-only design (Figure 4-1). In this case, the control group and experimental group are either performing at the exact same time or there is not a pre-program measurement. Measurements are taken after the program is implemented. The difference in the post-program performance of the two groups shows the amount of improvement that is directly related to the training program.

Figure 4-1. Post-Test Only, Control Group Design

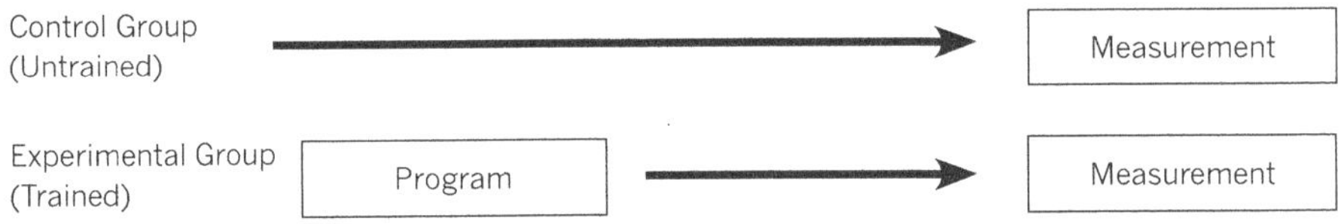

Isolate Program Impact

For the control group arrangement to be used, six conditions must be met:
1. One or two measures need to be identified that represent the outcome of the program. This is what is used to compare the control and experimental groups.
2. In addition to the talent development program, the factors that influence the outcome measures can be identified and the two groups are matched accordingly.
3. There are enough participants available from which to select the two groups.
4. The program training can be withheld from the control group without any operational problems.
5. The same environmental influences affect both groups during the experiment, with the talent development program being the only difference.
6. The experimental group is protected from contamination. In other words, the system for program implementation is such that members of the control group do not pick up and apply elements of the program.

If these conditions are met, there is a possibility for control group arrangement.

Case Study

Retail Merchandise Company (RMC) is a national chain of 420 stores. The executives at RMC were concerned about the slow sales growth and were experimenting with several programs to boost sales. One of their concerns focused on the interaction with customers. Sales associates were not actively involved in the sales process, usually waiting for a customer to make a purchasing decision and then proceeding with processing the sale. Several store managers had analyzed the situation to determine if more communication with the customer would boost sales. The analysis revealed that simple techniques to probe and guide the customer to a purchase should boost sales in each store.

The senior executives asked the talent development staff to experiment with a customer interactive skills program for a small group of sales associates. The training staff would prefer a program produced by an external supplier to avoid the cost of development, particularly if the program was not effective. The specific charge from the management team was to implement the program in three stores, monitor the results, and make recommendations.

The talent development staff selected an interactive selling skills program, which makes significant use of skill practices. The program includes two days of training in which participants have an opportunity to practice each of the skills with a fellow classmate, followed by three weeks of on-the-job application. Then, there's a final day of training that includes a discussion of problems, issues, barriers, and concerns about using the skills. Additional practice and fine-tuning of skills also take place in the final one-day session. At RMC, this program was tried in the electronics area of three stores, with 16 people trained in each store.

One of the most important parts of this evaluation is isolating the effects of the training program. This is a critical issue in the planning stage. The key question is, "When sales data are collected three months after the program is implemented, how much of the increase in sales, if any, is directly related to the program?" Although the improvement in sales may be linked to the talent development program, other nontraining factors contribute to improvement. Though the cause-and-effect relationship between training and performance improvement can be very confusing and difficult to prove, it can be accomplished with an acceptable degree of accuracy. In the planning process, the challenge is to develop one or more specific strategies to isolate the effects of training and include it on the ROI analysis plan.

In this case study, the issue was relatively easy to address. Senior executives gave the talent development staff the freedom to select any stores for implementation of the pilot program. The performance of the three stores selected for the program was compared with the performance of three other stores that were identical in every way possible. This approach represents the most accurate way to isolate the effects of a program. Although other strategies, such as trend line analysis and estimation, would have also been feasible, the control group analysis was selected because of the appropriateness of the situation and the credibility of the analysis. The challenge in using a control versus experimental group is to appropriately select both sets of stores.

Think About This

You have been tasked with developing the criteria to match the control and experimental groups in this case study. What are your criteria for matching the two groups?

- _____
- _____
- _____
- _____

It was important for those stores to be as identical as possible, so the talent development staff developed several criteria that could influence sales. This list became quite extensive and included market data, store-level data, management and leadership data, and individual differences. In a conference call with regional managers, this list was pared down to the four most likely influences. The executives selected those influences that would account for at least 80 percent of the differences in weekly store sales per associate. These criteria were as follows:

- **store size,** with the larger stores commanding a higher performance level
- **store location,** using a market variable of median household income in the area where customers live
- **customer traffic levels,** which measures the flow of traffic through the store; this measure was originally developed for security purposes
- **previous store performance,** a good predictor of future performance; the talent development staff collected six months of data on weekly sales per associate to identify the two groups.

While other factors could have had an influence on sales, there was up-front agreement that these four criteria would be used to select three stores for the pilot program and match them with three other stores. As a fallback position, in case the control group arrangement did not work, participant estimates were planned.

Disadvantages and Advantages

While the gold standard in demonstrating cause-and-effect relationships, the control group arrangement does have some inherent problems that may make it difficult to apply. First is that the process is inappropriate for many situations. For some types of talent development programs, it is not proper to withhold a program from one group while engaging another. This is particularly important for critical skills that are needed immediately on the job. For example, in entry-level training, employees need basic skills to perform their jobs. It would be improper to withhold training from a group of new employees just so they can be compared with a group that receives the training. Although this would reveal the effect of initial training, it would further handicap those individuals who are struggling to learn necessary skills and trying to cope with the job situation. Situations like the previous case study describing the use of control group to demonstrate improved store sales are feasible. The training provided was not necessarily essential to the job, and the organization was not completely convinced that it would add value to actual sales.

This barrier keeps many control groups from being implemented. Management is not willing to withhold a program in one area to see how it works in another. However, in practice, there are many opportunities for a naturally occurring control group to develop in situations where programs are implemented throughout an organization. If it will take several months for

Chapter 4

everyone to participate in a program, there may be enough time for a parallel comparison between the initial group and the last group. These naturally occurring control groups often exist in major talent development program implementations.

A second problem is that the control groups must be addressed early enough to influence the implementation schedule so that similar groups can be used in the comparison. Dozens of factors can affect employee performance, some of them individual and others contextual. To tackle the issue on a practical basis, it is best to select three to five variables that will have the greatest influence on performance.

A third problem with the control group arrangement is contamination, which can occur when participants in the program influence others in the control group. Sometimes the reverse situation occurs when members of the control group model the behavior from the trained group.

In either case, the experiment becomes contaminated because the influence of the program filters to the control group. This can be minimized by ensuring that control groups and experimental groups are at different locations, have different shifts, or are on different floors in the same building. When this is not possible, it is sometimes helpful to explain to both groups that one group will receive training now and another will receive training at a later date. Also, it may be helpful to appeal to the sense of responsibility of those being trained and ask them not to share the information with others.

 Noted

A challenge is when the control group outperforms the experimental group. In some cases, the program was, in fact, a poor solution to the opportunity. But more times than not, when the control group outperforms the experimental design, there is a problem with the research design. Therefore, it is important to have an alternative approach readily available to determine how much improvement is due the program.

Fourth, and closely related to the previous problem, is the issue of time. The longer a control group and experimental group comparison goes on, the greater the likelihood that other influences will affect the results. More variables will enter into the situation, contaminating the results. On the other end of the scale, there must be enough time so that a clear pattern can emerge between the two groups. Thus, the timing for control group arrangement must strike a delicate balance of waiting long enough for their performance differences to show but not so long that the results become seriously contaminated.

A fifth problem occurs when the different groups function under different environmental influences because they may be in different locations. Sometimes the selection of the groups can help prevent this problem from occurring. Also, using more groups than necessary and discarding those with some environmental differences is another tactic.

A sixth problem with using control groups is that it may appear to be too research oriented for the organization. For example, management may not want to take the time to experiment before proceeding with a program, or they may not want to withhold a program from a group just to measure the impact of an experimental program. Because of this concern, some professionals do not entertain the idea of using control groups. When the process is used, however, some organizations conduct it with pilot participants as the experimental group and nonparticipants as the control group. Under this arrangement, the control group is not informed of their control group status.

The primary advantage of using control versus experimental groups is that it is the gold standard in demonstrating cause and effect. This level of credibility is important when reporting results of a major talent development initiative. When the experimental and control groups are evenly matched and the program is the only other factor, it's difficult for someone to push back on results. In today's era of agility and analytics, experimentation is becoming more acceptable than in the past. Senior leaders recognize the need to pivot quickly if a program is not working; so, rather than invest in a complete rollout of an initiative, testing with a smaller group today can avoid a bad investment decision in the future.

Trend Line Analysis

Another technique used to isolate the impact of talent development programs is the forecasting and trend line analysis process. This approach has credibility if it is feasible and, when appropriate, is an alternative to control group arrangement.

A trend line is drawn using pre-program performance as a base and extending the trend into the future. After the program is conducted, actual performance is compared to the projected value, the trend line. Any improvement of performance over what the trend line predicted can then be reasonably attributed to the program. For this to work, four conditions must exist:

1. **Pre-program data are available.** These represent the impact data—the proposed outcome of the program. While the number of data points required to make a trend depends on the data, six data points would be the minimum.
2. **Pre-program data should be stable,** not erratic.

Chapter 4

3. **The trend that has developed prior to the program is expected to continue** if the program is not implemented to alter it.
4. **No other new variables enter the process** after the program is conducted. The key word is "new," realizing that the trend has been established because of the variables already in place, and no additional variables have entered the process beyond the talent development program.

Case Study

In a warehouse where documents are shipped to fill consumer orders, shipment productivity is routinely monitored. For one particular team, the shipment productivity is well below where the organization desires it to be. The ideal productivity level is 100 percent, reflecting that the actual shipments equal the scheduled shipments.

Figure 4-2. Trend Line of Productivity

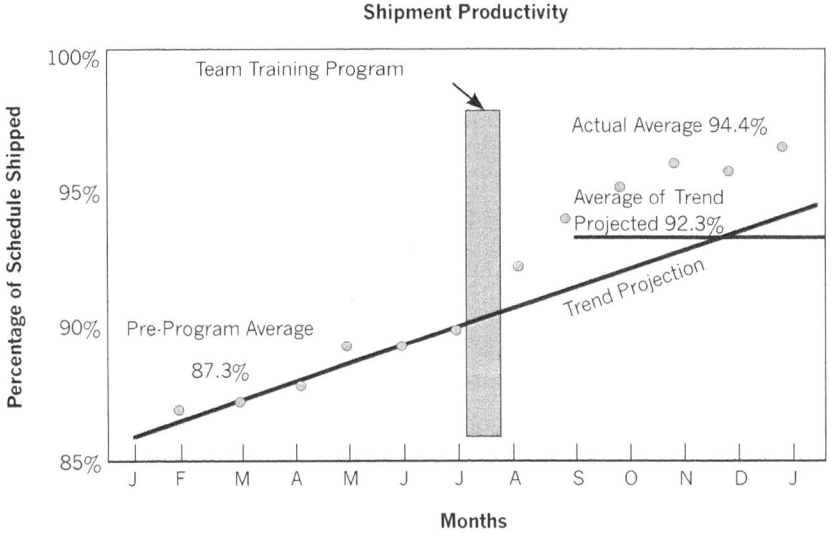

Figure 4-2 shows the data before and after the team training program. As shown in the figure, there was an upward trend on the data prior to conducting the training. Although the program apparently had a dramatic effect on shipment productivity, the trend line shows that improvement would have continued anyway, based on the trend that had been previously established. It is tempting to measure the improvement by comparing the average six months of shipments prior to the program (87.3 percent) to the actual average of six months after the program (94.4 percent), yielding a 7.1 percentage point difference. However, a more accurate comparison is the six-month actual average after the program (94.4 percent) compared with the trend line (92.3 percent); the difference is 2.1 percentage points. This comparison accounts for the trend (and all factors influencing the trend), as well as the program

If the variance of the data is high, the stability of the trend line becomes an issue. If this is an extremely critical issue and the stability cannot be assessed from a direct plot of the data, more detailed statistical analyses can be used to determine if the data are stable enough to make the projection. The trend line can be projected with a simple formula available in many calculators and software packages.

Disadvantages and Advantages

The primary disadvantage of the trend-line approach is that it is not always accurate. The use of this approach assumes that the events that influenced the performance variable prior to the program are still in place after the program, except for the implementation of the training program. Also, it assumes that no new influences entered the situation at the time the training was conducted. This is seldom the case.

The primary advantage of this approach is that it is simple and inexpensive. If historical data are available, a trend line can quickly be drawn and differences estimated. Although not exact, it does provide a quick assessment of a talent development program's potential results.

Mathematical Modeling

A more analytical approach to isolating program effects is the use of mathematical modeling. Correlation does not equal causation; this has been proven time and again. Yet, scientists continue to demonstrate approaches in which, under certain circumstances, correlational analysis indicates causal outcomes (Mooij et al. 2016). Through the development of models using robust statistical analysis, an evaluator can demonstrate a relatively reliable connection between performance variables. This approach represents a mathematical interpretation of the trend-line analysis when multiple variables enter the situation at the time of a program.

The basic premise is that the actual performance of a measure, related to talent development, is compared to movement of the measures related to other factors. A critical path is formed that can lead one to ascertain that some amount of improvement in the measure can be explained by

Chapter 4

a talent development program. This form of analysis is becoming more popular given the amount of data and technology now available. However, it is still not as accessible to evaluators of talent development as in other areas.

Case Study

A basic example of how this type of analysis can be employed is in a retail setting where two investments were being made to increase sales: advertising and training. The marketing and advertising team tracked investment in advertising and sales over time. Using the method of least squares, they found that there was a mathematical relationship between advertising and sales: $Y = 140 + 40X$, where Y represented the daily sales per employee and X represented the investment in advertising divided by 1,000. Prior to the program the average daily sales, using a one-month average, was $1,100. The investment in advertising was $24,000. In formula form: $1,100 = 140 + 40(24)$.

Six months after the program, average sales on a monthly basis was $1,500. Investment in advertising was $30,000. However, there had been a training program during that six months. While the senior executive and talent development team discussed other factors, they agreed the only other "significant" factor that could have influenced sales was the training program. To account for the increase, the first step was to solve for the contribution of advertising using the mathematical formula: $Y = 140 + 40(30)$. The output showed that average sales due to advertising was $1,340. The difference between the $1,500 and $1,340 was $160. This difference was attributed to the training program.

Disadvantages and Advantages

The major disadvantage with mathematical modeling occurs when several variables enter the process. The complexity of analytics multiplies, and the use of sophisticated statistical packages for multiple-variable analyses is necessary. Even then, a good fit of the data to the model may not be possible. Unfortunately, some organizations have not developed mathematical relationships for output variables as a function of one or more inputs. Without them, this approach is difficult to use.

The primary advantage of this type of analysis is that more organizations are investing in development of analytics capability. With this capability and the use of robust analysis, it is becoming more accessible to make accurate predictions of organization performance measures with and without talent development programs.

Expert Estimation

An easily implemented method to isolate the effect of learning is to obtain information directly from experts who understand the business performance measures. The experts could be any number of individuals, including participants, supervisors, managers, sponsors, subject matter experts, process owners, external experts, and customers. For many programs, the participants are the experts. After all, the measure is reflecting their individual performance. They may know more about the relationships between the different factors, including learning, than any other individual.

Because of the importance of estimations from program participants, much of the discussion in this section relates to how to collect this information directly from participants. The same methods would be used to collect data from others. The effectiveness of the approach rests on the assumption that participants are capable of determining how much of a performance improvement is related to the training program. Because their actions have produced the improvement, participants may have very accurate input on the issue. Although an estimate, this value will typically have credibility with management because participants are at the center of the change or improvement.

When using this technique, four assumptions are made:

1. A talent development program has been conducted with a variety of different activities, exercises, and learning opportunities, all focused on improving performance.
2. Business measures have been identified prior to the program and have been monitored following the program. Data monitoring has revealed an improvement in the business measure. (The process starts with this step.)
3. There is a need to link the talent development program to the specific amount of performance improvement and develop the monetary effect of the improvement. This information forms the basis for calculating the actual ROI.
4. The participants are capable of providing knowledgeable input on the cause-and-effect relationship between the different factors, including learning and the output measure.

With these assumptions, the participants can pinpoint the results linked to the program and provide data necessary to develop the ROI. This can be accomplished by using a focus group or a questionnaire.

Focus Group Approach

The focus group approach works extremely well for this challenge if the group size is relatively small—in the eight to 12 range. If much larger, the groups should be divided into multiple groups. Focus groups provide the opportunity for members to share information equally, avoiding domination by any one individual. The process taps the input, creativity, and reactions of the entire group.

The focus group session should take about one hour (slightly more if there are multiple factors affecting the results or there are multiple business measures). The facilitator should be neutral to the process (that is, the same individual conducting the program should not conduct this focus group).

The task is to link a talent development program to business performance. The group is presented with the improvement, and they provide input on how much of the improvement is due to the program. Twelve steps are recommended to arrive at the most credible value for learning impact:

1. **Explain the task.** The first step is to describe the task to members of the focus group. Participants should be clear that there has been improvement in performance. While many factors could have contributed to the performance, the task of this group is to determine how much of the improvement is related to the specific program.

2. **Discuss the rules.** Each participant should be encouraged to provide input, limiting comments to two minutes per person for any specific issue. Comments are confidential and will not be linked to a specific individual.

3. **Explain the importance of the process.** The participant's role in the process is critical. Because it is their new actions, behaviors, or processes that have led to performance improvement in measures related to their work, they are in the best position to indicate what has caused this improvement; they are the experts in this process. Without quality input, the contribution of the program (or any other processes) may never be known.

4. **Select the first measure and show the improvement.** Using actual data, show the level of performance prior to and following the program; in essence, the change in business results is reported. If the participants have individual data, the individual improvements should be used.

5. **Identify the different factors that have contributed to the performance.** Using input from experts and process owners—others who are knowledgeable about the improvements—identify the factors that have influenced the improvement (for example, the volume of work has changed, a new system has been implemented, or technology has been enhanced). If these are known, they are listed as the factors that may have contributed to the performance improvement.
6. **Identify other factors that have contributed to the performance.** In some situations, only the participants know other influencing factors, and those factors should surface at this time.
7. **Discuss the linkage.** Taking each factor one at a time, the participants individually describe the linkage between that factor and the results using a time limit of two minutes. For example, for the program influence, the participants would describe how the program has driven the actual improvement by providing examples, anecdotes, and other supporting evidence. Participants may require some prompting to provide comments. If they cannot provide dialogue on this issue, there's a good chance that that factor had no influence.
8. **Repeat the process for each factor.** Each factor that could have influenced performance in the measure is explored until all the participants have discussed the linkage between all the factors and the business performance improvement. After this linkage has been discussed, the participants should have a clear understanding of the cause-and-effect relationship between the various factors and the business improvement.
9. **Allocate the improvement.** Participants are asked to allocate the percentage of improvement to each of the factors discussed. Participants are provided a pie chart that represents a total amount of improvement for the measure in question and are asked to carve up the pie, allocating the percentages to different improvements with a total of 100 percent. Some participants may feel uncertain with this process but should be encouraged to complete it using their best estimate. Uncertainty will be addressed later in the meeting.
10. **Provide a confidence estimate.** The participants are then asked to review the allocation percentages and, for each one, estimate their level of confidence in the allocation estimate. Using a scale of 0 to 100 percent, where 0 percent represents no confidence and 100 percent is complete certainty, participants express their

level of certainty with their estimates in the previous step. A participant may be more comfortable with some factors than others, so the confidence estimate may vary. This confidence estimate serves as a vehicle to adjust results.

11. **Ask the participants to multiply the two percentages.** For example, if an individual has allocated 35 percent of the improvement to learning and is 80 percent confident, they would multiply 35 percent by 80 percent, which is 28 percent. In essence, the participant is suggesting that at least 28 percent of the business improvement is linked to the talent development program. The confidence estimate serves as a conservative discount factor, adjusting for the error of the estimate. The pie charts with the calculations are collected without names, and the calculations are verified. Another option is to collect the pie charts and make the calculations for the participants.

12. **Report results.** If possible, the average of the adjusted values is developed and communicated to the group. Also, the summary of all the information should be communicated to the participants as soon as possible. Participants who do not provide information are excluded from the analysis.

Table 4-1 illustrates the focus group estimation approach with an example of one participant's estimates. This participant allocates 50 percent of the improvement to the talent development program. The confidence percentage is a reflection of possible error in the estimate. A 70 percent confidence level equates to a potential error range of ±30 percent (100 percent × 70 percent = 30 percent). The 50 percent allocation to the program represents ±15 percent (50 percent × 30 percent = 15 percent). Thus, the contribution could be 65 percent (50 percent + 15 percent = 65 percent) or 35 percent (50 percent − 15 percent = 35 percent) or somewhere in between.

The participant's allocation is in the range of 35 to 65 percent. In essence, the confidence estimate frames this error range. To be conservative, the lower side of the range is used (35 percent).

This approach is equivalent to multiplying the factor estimate by the confidence percentage to develop a usable learning factor value of 35 percent. This adjusted percentage is then multiplied by the actual amount of the improvement (post-program minus pre-program value) to isolate the portion attributed to the program. The adjusted improvement is now ready for conversion to monetary values and, ultimately, for use in developing the return on investment.

Table 4-1. Example of a Participant's Estimation

Factor That Influenced Improvement		Percentage of Improvement	Percentage of Confidence Expressed	Adjusted Percentage of Improvement
1. Talent development program		50%	70%	35%
2. Change in procedures		10%	80%	8%
3. Adjustment in standards		10%	50%	5%
4. Revision to incentive plan		20%	90%	18%
5. Increased management attention		10%	50%	5%
	Total	100%		

This approach provides a credible way to isolate the effects of the program when other methods will not work. It is often regarded as the low-cost solution to the problem because it takes only a few focus groups and a small amount of time to arrive at this conclusion. In most of these settings, the actual conversion to monetary value is not conducted by the group but developed in another way. For most data, the monetary value may already exist as a standard, acceptable value. However, if the participants must provide input on the value of the data, it can be approached in the same focus group meeting as another phase of the process in which the participants provide input into the actual monetary value of the unit. To reach an accepted value, the steps are very similar to the steps for isolation.

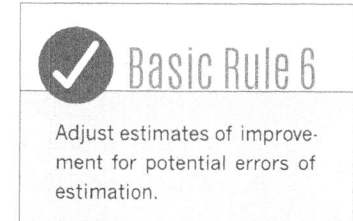

Basic Rule 6

Adjust estimates of improvement for potential errors of estimation.

Questionnaire Approach

Sometimes focus groups are not available or are considered unacceptable for use in data collection. The participants may not be available for a group meeting, or the focus groups may become too expensive. In these situations, it may be helpful to collect similar information via a questionnaire. With this approach, participants address the same issues as those addressed in the focus group, but now on a series of impact questions imbedded in a follow-up questionnaire.

The questionnaire may focus solely on isolating the effects of talent development, as detailed in the previous example, or it may focus on the monetary value derived from the program, with the isolation issue being only a part of the data collected. Using questionnaires is a more versatile approach when it is not certain exactly how participants will provide impact data. In some programs, the precise measures that will be influenced by the program may not be known. This is sometimes the case in programs involving leadership, team building, communications, negotiations, problem solving, innovation, and other types of talent development initiatives. In these situations, it is helpful to obtain information from participants on a series of impact questions, showing how they have used what they have learned and how the work unit has been affected. It is important for participants to know about these questions before they receive the questionnaire; otherwise, they may not respond or may struggle with their responses.

The following is a series of questions that will lead to determining the improvement in impact measures due to the program and the value of that improvement. Questions 8, 9, and 10 are those necessary to isolate program effects on performance improvement.

1. How have you and your job changed as a result of attending this program (knowledge and skills application)?
2. What effects do these changes bring to your work or work unit?
3. How is this effect measured (specific measure)?
4. How much did this measure change after you participated in the program (monthly, weekly, or daily amount)?
5. What is the unit value of the measure?
6. What is the basis for this unit value? Please indicate the assumption made and the specific calculations you performed to arrive at the value.
7. What is the annual value of this change or improvement in the work unit (for the first year)?
8. Recognizing that many other factors influence output results in addition to the program, please identify the other factors that could have contributed to this performance.
9. What percentage of this improvement can be attributed directly to the application of skills and knowledge gained in the program? (0 percent to 100 percent)
10. What confidence do you have in the above estimate and data, expressed as a percentage? (0 percent = no confidence; 100 percent = complete certainty)
11. What other individuals or groups could estimate this percentage or determine the amount?

Case Study

Perhaps an illustration of this process can reveal its effectiveness and acceptability. In a large global organization, the impact of a leadership program for new managers was being assessed. Because the decision to calculate the impact of the program was made after the program had been conducted, control group arrangement was not feasible as a method to isolate the effects of training. Also, before the program was implemented, no specified impact data were identified as directly linked to the program. Participants may drive one or more of a dozen business performance measures. Consequently, it was not appropriate to use trend line analysis. Participants' estimates proved to be the most useful way to assess the impact of the program on performance improvement. In a detailed follow-up questionnaire, participants were asked a variety of questions regarding the applications of what was learned from the program. As part of the program, the individuals were asked to develop action plans and implement them, although there was no specific follow-up plan needed.

Although this series of questions is challenging, when set up properly and presented to participants in an appropriate way, it can be very effective for collecting impact data. Table 4-2 shows a sample of the calculations from these questions for this particular program.

Although this is an estimate, the approach has credibility. Four adjustments are effectively used with this method to reflect a conservative approach:

- The individuals who do not respond to the questionnaire or provide usable data on the questionnaire are assumed to have no improvements. This is probably an understatement of results because some individuals will have improvements but not report them on the questionnaire.
- Extreme data and incomplete, unrealistic, and unsupported claims are omitted from the analysis, although they may be included in the intangible benefits.
- Because only annualized values are used, it is assumed that there are no benefits from the program after the first year of implementation. In reality, leadership development should be expected to add value for several years after the program has been conducted.
- The confidence level, expressed as a percentage, is multiplied by the improvement value to reduce the amount of the improvement by the potential error.

Basic Rule 7

If no improvement data are available for a population or from a specific source, it is assumed that little or no improvement has occurred.

Chapter 4

When presented to senior management, the results of this study were perceived to be an understatement of the program's success. The data and the process were considered to be credible and accurate.

Table 4-2. Sample of Input From Participants in a Leadership Program for New Managers

Participant Number	Annual Improvement Value	Basis for Value	Confidence	Isolation Factor	Adjusted Value
11	$36,000	Improvement in efficiency of group. $3,000 per month × 12 (group estimate)	85%	50%	$15,300
42	$90,000	Turnover reduction. Two turnover statistics per year. Base salary × 1.5 = 45,000	90%	40%	$32,400
74	$24,000	Improvement in customer response time (8 to 6 hours). Estimated value: $2,000 per month	60%	55%	$7,920
55	$2,000	5% improvement in individual effectiveness ($40,500 × 5%)	75%	50%	$750
96	$10,000	Absenteeism reduction (50 absences per year × $200)	85%	75%	$6,375
117	$8,090	Team project completed 10 days ahead of schedule. Annual salaries: $210,500 = $809 per day × 10 days	90%	45%	$3,276
118	$159,000	Under budget for the year by this amount	100%	30%	$47,700
				Total	$113,721

Collecting an adequate amount of quality data from the series of impact questions is the critical challenge with this process. Participants must be primed to provide data, and this can be accomplished in six ways.

Basic Rule 8

Avoid use of extreme data items and unsupported claims when calculating ROI.

- Participants should know in advance that they are expected to provide this type of data along with an explanation of why the information is needed and how it will be used.
- Ideally, participants should see a copy of this questionnaire and discuss it while they are involved in the program. If possible, a verbal commitment to provide the data should be obtained at that time.

- Participants could be reminded of the requirement prior to the time to collect data. The reminder should come from others involved in the process—even the immediate manager.
- Participants could be provided with examples of how the questionnaire can be completed, using likely scenarios and types of data.
- The immediate manager could coach participants through the process.
- The immediate manager could review and approve the data.

These steps help keep the data collection process with its chain of impact questions from being a surprise. It will also accomplish three critical tasks:

- **The response rate will increase.** Because participants commit to provide data during the session, a greater percentage will respond.
- **The quantity of data will improve.** Participants will understand the chain of impact and understand how data will be used. They will complete more questions.
- **The quality of the data is enhanced.** With up-front expectations, there is greater understanding of the type of data needed and improved confidence in the data provided. Perhaps subconsciously, participants begin to think through consequences of training and specific result measures.

Basic Rule 9

Use only the first year of annual benefits in ROI analysis of short-term solutions

Disadvantages and Advantages

Participant estimation is a useful technique to isolate the effect of talent development; however, the process has some disadvantages. It is an estimate and, consequently, does not have the accuracy desired by some talent development managers. Also, the input data may be unreliable because some participants are incapable of providing these types of estimates. They might not be aware of exactly which factors contributed to the results or they may be reluctant to provide data. If the questions come as a surprise, the data will be scarce.

Several advantages make this strategy attractive. It is a simple process, easily understood by most participants and by others who review evaluation data. It is inexpensive, takes very little time and analysis, and thus results in an efficient addition to the evaluation process. Estimates originate from a credible source—the individuals who produced the improvement.

The advantages seem to offset the disadvantages. Isolating the effects of talent development will never be precise, but this estimate may be accurate enough for most clients and management groups. The process is appropriate when the participants are managers, supervisors, team leaders, sales associates, engineers, and other professional and technical employees.

This technique is the fallback isolation strategy when other techniques will not work. It is a fallback approach for when the effects of learning must be isolated and no other technique is feasible. Trainers, training managers, learning specialists, and performance improvement specialists are often reluctant to use a technique that lacks absolute precision. However, the primary audience for the data (the sponsor or senior manager) will readily accept this approach. Accepting the ambiguity with which decisions must sometimes be made, they understand estimates and that they may be the only way to connect a program with performance measures. They understand the challenge and appreciate the conservative approach, often commenting that the actual value is probably greater than the value presented. When organizations begin to use this routinely, it sometimes becomes the method of choice for isolation.

Data Collection From Other Experts

The previous approaches describe how data are collected from participants in the programs. Both the focus group approach and the questionnaire approach can be helpful in collecting data from others. Sometimes the supervisor of program participants may be capable of providing input on the extent of talent development's role in performance improvement. In some settings, the participants' supervisors may be more familiar with the other factors influencing performance. Consequently, they may be better equipped to provide estimates of impact. A word of caution: If the supervisors are physically removed from the actual settings, it may be difficult for them to understand the impact of talent development.

Managers may be asked to provide input, but only if they have some credible insight into the cause-and-effect relationship of these factors. If they are physically removed from the situation, they may not be very credible. Other possible sources of contributions include input from customers, external experts, the program sponsor, and any other group or individual who may be knowledgeable of these relationships.

Building Credibility With the Process

Isolating program effects is the most significant credibility step in the ROI Methodology. It is important to look more closely at issues around selecting techniques and strengthening credibility of the technique.

Selecting the Techniques

Table 4-3 shows the frequency with which each technique was selected as being applied by more than 200 best practice organizations that have been applying the ROI Methodology for five years or more. This table presents a high percentage level for comparison group analysis; the average use of this method in all impact studies would be significantly less. After all, these are best practice organizations, and they have worked diligently to use the most credible analyses. The 20 percent representing "Other" is a variety of techniques that are less likely to be used.

Table 4-3. Best Practice Use of Techniques

Isolating the Effects of Talent Development Programs

Method[1]	Best Practice Use[2]
1. Control group arrangement	35%
2. Trend line analysis	20%
3. Expert estimation	50%
4. Other	20%

1. Listed in order of credibility.
2. Percentages exceed 100 percent.

With several techniques available to isolate the impact of learning, selecting the most appropriate techniques for the specific program can be difficult. Estimates are simple and inexpensive, while others are more time consuming and costly. When attempting to make the selection decision, several factors should be considered:

- feasibility of the technique
- accuracy provided with the technique, when compared to the accuracy needed
- credibility of the technique with the target audience
- specific cost to implement the technique
- the amount of disruption in normal work activities as the technique is implemented
- participant, staff, and management time needed with the particular technique.

Using Multiple Techniques

Multiple techniques or sources of data input should be considered because two sources are usually better than one. When multiple sources are used, a conservative method is recommended to combine the inputs. A conservative approach builds acceptance and credibility.

The target audience should always be provided with explanations of the process and the various subjective factors involved. Multiple sources allow an organization to experiment with different techniques and build confidence with a particular technique. For example, if management is concerned about the accuracy of participants' estimates, a combination of a control group and participants' estimates could be attempted to check the accuracy of the estimation process.

Strengthening Credibility

It is not unusual for the ROI in talent development to be high. Even when a portion of the improvement is allocated to other factors, the numbers are still impressive in many situations. The audience should understand that, although every effort was made to isolate the impact, it is still a figure that is not precise and may contain error. It represents the best estimate of the impact given the constraints, conditions, and resources available.

One way to strengthen the credibility of the ROI is to consider the different factors that influence the credibility of data. Table 4-4 is a listing of typical factors that influence the credibility of data presented to a particular group. The issue of isolating the effects of the talent development program is influenced by several of these credibility factors.

The reputation of the source of the data is important to consider. The most knowledgeable expert must provide input and be involved in the analysis in this topic. Also, the motives of the researchers can have a major influence on perceived credibility. A third party must facilitate any focus group that is done, and the data must be collected objectively. In addition, the assumptions made in the analysis and the methodology of the study should be clearly defined so that the audience will understand the steps taken to increase the credibility. The type of data focuses directly on the impact data: The data have changed, and the challenge is to isolate the effects on that change. Managers prefer to deal with hard data, typically collected from the output of most programs. Finally, by isolating the effects of only one program, the scope of analysis is kept narrow, enhancing the credibility.

Table 4-4. Factors That Influence the Credibility of Data

• Reputation of the source of the data	• Personal bias of audience	• Realism of the outcome data
• Reputation of the source of the study	• Methodology of the study	• Type of data
• Motives of the researchers	• Assumptions made in the analysis	• Scope of analysis

Getting It Done

In chapter 2, you were introduced to the data collection plan and the ROI analysis plan. In chapter 3, you completed the data collection plan for a program you plan to evaluate to ROI. Here is where you begin completing the ROI analysis plan.

Table 4-5 provides a blank ROI analysis plan. Transfer your Level 4 measures from your data collection plan to the first column of the ROI analysis plan. Then, identify the techniques you will use to isolate the effects of the program from other influences and write the techniques in the second column aligned with each Level 4 measure. Remember, this step must be taken, so a technique should be included for each objective.

In the next chapter, you will continue completing the ROI analysis plan.

Chapter 4

Table 4-5. ROI Analysis Plan

Program: _____ Responsibility: _____ Date: _____

Data Items (Usually w/Level 4)	Methods for Isolating the Effects of the Program	Methods of Converting Data to Monetary Values	Cost Categories	Intangible Benefits	Communication Targets for Final Report	Other Influences or Issues During Application	Comments

110

5

Calculate ROI

What's Inside This Chapter

To continue building credibility for your talent development programs, you need to demonstrate the economic value they add to the organization. Specifically, in this chapter you will learn the basic steps to move from Level 4 to Level 5 by:

- converting data to monetary value
- tabulating fully loaded costs
- calculating the ROI.

5

Calculate ROI

Converting Data to Monetary Value

The fundamental difference between Level 4 and Level 5 begins with converting the benefits of the program (Level 4) to monetary value. For some, this is a frightening task; others recognize that if standard values for the measures are unavailable, there are other techniques to convert measures to money.

Level 4 measures are defined as the consequence of applying knowledge and skills (Level 3) learned in a program. These consequences result in measures categorized as hard data and soft data. But what do these categories really mean?

Hard Data Versus Soft Data

Hard data include measures that are easy to collect and measure, quantifiable, easy to convert to monetary value, objectively based, common measures of organizations performance, and immediately credible with management. They are the primary measurements of improvement, presented in rational, undisputed facts. Hard data include measures of output, quality, cost, and time.

Every organization, private, public, social, or academic, has some form of these measures. Table 5-1 provides examples of measures representing hard data. Although not all-inclusive, this list should cover some measures tracked by your organization.

On the other hand, soft data represent measures that are difficult to measure, difficult to quantify, subjectively based, less credible as performance measures, and behaviorally oriented. The measures, although important, are often perceived as less reliable when measuring performance, due to an inherent level of subjectivity. Soft data include measures such as work habits, new skills, climate, development, satisfaction, and initiative.

Every organization has some measure that can be categorized as soft data. Table 5-2 presents examples of each category.

Table 5-1. Hard Data

Output	Quality
Units produced	Errors
Tons manufactured	Waste
Items assembled	Rejects
Reports processed	Rework
Students graduated	Shortages
Research grants awarded	Defects
Tasks completed	Failures
Number of shipments	Malicious intrusions
New accounts generated	Accidents
Cost	**Time**
Budget variances	Cycle time
Unit costs	Response time
Variable costs	Equipment downtime
Overhead costs	Overtime
Operating costs	Processing time
Penalties/fines	Supervisory time
Project cost savings	Meeting time
Accident costs	Work stoppages
Sales expense	Order response time

Table 5-2. Soft Data

Work Habits	New Skills
Absenteeism	Decisions made
Tardiness	Problems solved
First aid treatments	Grievances resolved
Safety violations	Conflicts avoided
Communication	Interaction with staff
Climate	**Development**
Number of grievances	Number of promotions
Employee complaints	Number of pay increases
Employee engagement	Requests for transfer
Organizational commitment	Performance appraisal ratings
Employee turnover	Job effectiveness
Satisfaction	**Initiative**
Job satisfaction	Implementation of new ideas
Customer satisfaction	Innovation
Employee loyalty	Goals achieved
Increased confidence	Completion of projects

Chapter 5

> ### Think About This
>
> Select whether you think the measure represents hard data or soft data. What is improvement in the measure worth?
>
> | Objective | Hard | Soft |
> |---|---|---|
> | Decrease error rates on reports by 20 percent. | ❏ | ❏ |
> | Decrease the amount of time required to complete a project. | ❏ | ❏ |
> | Increase the customer satisfaction index by 25 percent in three months. | ❏ | ❏ |
> | Reduce litigation costs by 24 percent. | ❏ | ❏ |
> | Improve teamwork. | ❏ | ❏ |
> | Enhance creativity. | ❏ | ❏ |
> | Increase the number of new patents. | ❏ | ❏ |
> | Reduce absenteeism. | ❏ | ❏ |

Tangible Versus Intangible Data

Many readers consider measures like customer satisfaction, teamwork, creativity, and absenteeism as soft data items. Do you? Now, think about this:

- If customer satisfaction is a soft measure, then how are quantitative values assigned to it to create a customer satisfaction index? Do you place numbers on (or quantify) customer satisfaction?
- If executives apply their newly acquired leadership skills and you find that there is increased teamwork, why do you care? You hope it yields greater productivity leading to increased sales and reduced costs.
- Why does it matter if your staff is more creative? Through the use of creative thinking, your product development meetings are more efficient.
- If an absence is a soft measure, then how do you track it? Is someone monitoring how many days employees fail to show up for work?

Many people suggest that hard data represent tangible measures; others suggest that soft data represent intangibles. However, whether hard or soft, improvement in the measures lead to a quantified output that can then lead to economic value add, just like accountants may categorize products sold as tangible and services sold as intangible. In the end, both products and services are directly connected to revenue (and hopefully profit) for the organization. A better delineation of tangible and intangible measures is not whether they are objectively based (hard data) or subjectively based (soft data), but whether they are converted to money.

> There are five levels of data. Intangible benefits are impact data not converted to money. They represent a sixth type of data when reporting an ROI due to their importance to the organization.

All data can be converted to monetary value. As shown in Figure 5-1, this is done by tying measures to either cost savings and avoidance or revenue converted to profit.

Though all measures can be converted to money, several factors should be considered. One factor is the cost to convert the measure. You should not spend more on data conversion than the evaluation itself. Importance of the measure is another consideration. Some measures, such as customer satisfaction and employee satisfaction, stand alone quite well. When that is the case, you might think twice before attempting to convert the measure to money. A third consideration is credibility. While most business decisions are made on somewhat subjective data, the source of the data, the perceived bias behind the data, and the motive in presenting the results are all concerns when data are somewhat questionable. Don't risk credibility just to calculate an ROI. Intangible measures of success may be where you stop.

Figure 5-1. Data Conversion

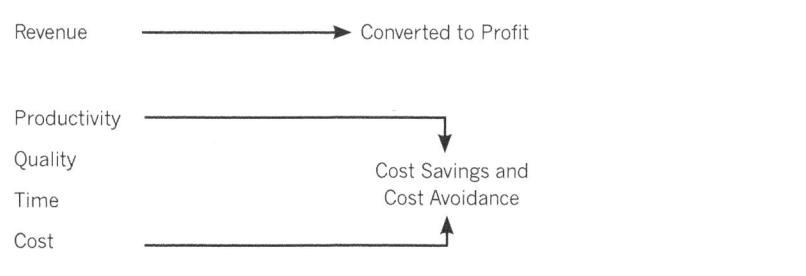

> **Think About This**
>
> Rank the following research results in order of credibility based on your definition of credibility. Have a colleague do the same. Compare your rankings and discuss why you ranked the items as you did. These are likely the same considerations others will give to your evaluation projects. Rank: 1 = most credible and 4 = least credible.
>
> | Research | Rank |
> |---|---|
> | Fatigued workers cost employers $136 billion per year.
Source: Fareed Zakaria, CNN Global Public Square, June 9, 2019. | |
> | Vulcan Materials Company produced 195 million tons of crushed stone during 2018.
Source: Annual Report. | |
> | IAMGOLD showed an ROI of 345 percent on a leadership program involving first-level managers.
Source: Parker, L., and C. Hubble. 2015. "Measuring ROI in a Supervisory Leadership Development Program." In Measuring the Success of Leadership Development, by P.P. Phillips, J.J. Phillips, and R.L. Ray. Alexandria, VA: ATD Press. | |
> | St. Mary-Corwin's Farm Stand Prescription Pantry saved money for the organization and avoided medical costs for recipients of service so much so that it resulted in a 650 percent ROI.
Source: Phillips, P.P., J.J. Phillips, G. Paone, and C.H. Gaudet. 2019. Value for Money: How to Show the Value for Money for All Types of Projects and Programs. Hoboken, NJ: John Wiley & Sons. | |

Data Conversion Methods

There are variety of techniques available to convert a measure to monetary value (listed in Table 5-3 in order of credibility). The success in converting data to monetary value is knowing what values are currently available. If values are not available, how best can you develop them? The first three techniques represent standard values. These are by far the most credible, because they are data that have been accepted by the organization. Following those are alternative techniques, which can also lead to credible values for the measures that matter.

Table 5-3. Techniques for Data Conversion

• Standard values 　» Output to contribution 　» Cost of quality 　» Employee's time	• Historical costs • Internal and external experts • External databases • Linking with other measures	• Estimations 　» Participants' estimates 　» Supervisors' and managers' estimates 　» Talent development staff estimates

Standard Values

Many organizations have standard values for measures of turnover, productivity, and quality. Organizations that use Six Sigma have a plethora of measures and, along with them, the monetary values of those measures. Look around your organization. Talk to people and see what is being measured in other parts of the organization. Borrow from those other departments and functions. If a measure has had a monetary value developed and accepted by the organization, there is no reason for you to reinvent it. Take advantage of the work of others.

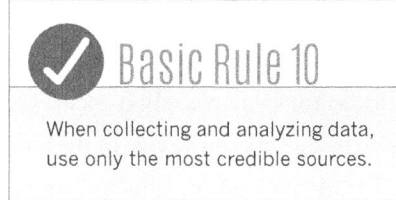

Basic Rule 10

When collecting and analyzing data, use only the most credible sources.

Standard values are grouped into three categories: output to contribution, cost of quality, and employees' time. When considering output to contribution, look at the value of an additional output. For example, organizations that work on a profit basis consider the marginal profit contribution in monetizing an additional sale. Think about Starbucks. The primary driver for customers coming to Starbucks is coffee. However, as you have noticed, there are cups, mugs, travel mugs, coffee grinders, and elaborate coffee pots, not to mention biscotti, chocolate, bottled water, juices, and milk. What if, you, as store manager, find that these other items are not moving off the shelf as quickly as expected? You, along with other store managers, attend a one-week program to learn about these products and develop skills that will help you sell more products along with the coffee. Six months after the program, a comprehensive evaluation is conducted, and you find that there has been an increase in sales in these peripheral products. The output is the increased sale. The contribution to the company, however, is the profit from the sale. Most organizations have a gross profit margin on sales readily available.

Another example of converting output data to contribution is with productivity measures. Organizations that are performance driven rather than profit driven have a variety of data that represent productivity. The idea here is increasing the production or processing of one more item at no additional cost, thus saving the company money equivalent to the unit cost of processing or producing that item.

Let's say you work at a passport office, and your entire role is to process passports. If you can process one more passport, given the resources and time you have available, the value of that one passport is equivalent to the cost of processing one passport. This one additional output—the passport—times the cost of processing the passport is the monetary contribution of increasing the output to the organization.

Now, consider the cost of quality, another standard value in organizations, especially in manufacturing and service firms. Placing the monetary value on some measures of quality is quite easy. For example, waste, reject rates, and defects are often monitored in organizations and already have a monetary value placed on them. Other measures, such as rework, can be converted to monetary value by looking at the cost of the work. For example, when employees make mistakes and errors in reporting, the cost (or value) of those mistakes is the cost incurred in reworking the report.

 Think About This

Using salary plus benefits as the basis for placing value on time for all positions enables you to standardize your approach. One caveat in this approach is when working with commissioned salespeople. The value of their work is ultimately the profit gain for the sales they make. However, if they are selling services or products that add no profit (for example, loss leaders), there is no direct value added by selling that specific product or service. When treating their time as money, use their average commission. This will ensure you capture value for their time and in such a way that it can be standardized across all commission sales positions. If they are paid base plus commission, use their salary plus benefits plus commission as the basis for time value.

The third category of standard value is employee time, probably the simplest and most basic approach to data conversion. If time is saved due to a program, the first question to ask is, "Whose time is it?" Then, convert time to monetary value by multiplying hourly salary plus the percentage of additional value for employee benefits (the human resources department can provide the benefits factor). A word of caution: When considering employee time as a benefit, the time savings is only realized when the amount of time saved is actually used for productive work. So, if a manager saves time by reducing the number of ineffective meetings the manager attends, the time saved should be applied to more work that is productive.

Historical Costs

When no standard values exist, look for historical costs. These are costs for which there is a receipt, so to speak. Using this technique often requires more time and effort than desired. In the end, however, you can develop a credible value for a given measure.

An example of using historical costs is the case of a sexual harassment prevention program that was implemented in a large health care organization. The measure of the investigation was formal, internal complaints. The value of the complaint was determined by looking at the historical cost of a complaint. These historical costs included litigation costs, legal fees and expenses, settlement losses, and costs of the investigation and defense of the organization. The cost of each of these was developed based on previous costs incurred by the organization for each complaint. Following the prevention program and at the end of the evaluation period, it was discovered that the organization had prevented 14.8 complaints due to the program. (This is after isolating other variables.) The monetary value for one complaint based on historical costs was then multiplied by the number of complaints reduced for the year due to the program.

Internal and External Experts

When standard values are unavailable and developing the monetary values through historical costs is not feasible, the next option is to go to internal or external experts. Using this approach, ask the expert to provide the cost for the value of one unit of improvement for the measure under investigation. Internal experts have knowledge of the situation and the respect of management; external experts are well published and have the respect of the larger community. In either case, keep in mind that these experts have their own methods to develop the values. Therefore, it's important for the experts to understand your intent and the measure for which you want to develop the monetary value.

An example of using an internal expert to provide monetary value for a measure is in looking at the electric utility industry. All electric utility companies have on staff an expert in the development of rates. When a utility adjusts rates—either raising or lowering rates—the monetary effect of that adjustment needs to be considered. This often falls to the economist. If rates were being manipulated, the executive staff calls the expert and asks for the estimate for the economic impact of the rate adjustment.

External Databases

Sometimes there are no standard values, no receipts, and no expertise. When this is the case, go to databases. Today, more than any time in the past, talent development professionals have good research at their fingertips. External databases provide a variety of information, including the monetary value of an array of measures. Take the use of external databases to convert a measure to monetary value in the case of turnover. A company implemented a stress management program, which was driven by the excessive turnover due to the stress that came from changing a bureaucratic, sluggish organization into a competitive force in the marketplace. After implementing the stress management program, turnover was reduced along with improvements in other measures, such as productivity and job satisfaction. In calculating the ROI, the evaluators went to a variety of databases to determine the value of turnover

Chapter 5

for a particular employee leaving the organization. The turnover studies used in the research revealed that a value of 85 percent of the annual base pay is what it was costing the organization for the people in this job classification to leave. While senior managers thought the cost of turnover was slightly overstated using the databases, it did give them a basis from which to begin determining the value of this measure.

Linking With Other Measures

When standard values, historical costs, and internal or external experts are not available and external databases do not provide the information that you need, another technique to convert a measure to monetary value is linking the value of that measure with other measures that have already been converted to monetary values. This approach involves identifying existing relationships showing a correlation between the measure under investigation and another measure to which a standard value has been applied. In some situations, the relationship between more than two measures is connected. Ultimately, this chain of measures is traced to a monetary value often based on profits. Keep in mind that the further you get from the actual monetary value, the greater the assumptions built in and the lower the credibility of the information. Using a methodology to link measures to other measures that have been converted to monetary value is often sufficient for converting measures when calculating the ROI of talent development programs.

 Think About This

Effective database research takes time. Consider the following steps to help reduce time and increase effectiveness of your search:
1. Select a database that aligns with the measures you are trying to convert to money.
2. Formulate a specific research question or objective.
3. Define the key words in the research question.
4. Identify synonyms for the key words, just to ensure you get complete coverage on the topic.
5. Search your databases.

Keep track of your findings. It may even be helpful to document them in a software application database so you can easily reference them in the future. If you don't have time to search, call a librarian!

Estimations

When the previous methods are inappropriate and you still want to convert a measure to monetary value, use an estimation process that has been proven conservative and credible with executives in your organization. The estimates of monetary value can come from participants, supervisors, managers, and even the talent development staff. The process of using estimation to convert a measure to monetary value is quite simple. The data can be gathered through focus groups, interviews, or questionnaires (discussed in chapter 3). The key is clearly defining the measure so that those who are asked to provide the estimate have a clear understanding of that measure.

The first step in the estimation approach is to determine who is the most credible source of the data. Typically, the participants realize the contribution they are making to the organization after participating in a talent development program. But, depending on what job group those participants work in, you might develop data that are more credible if you go to the supervisors or managers. Only fall back on the talent development staff when you have no other option and are under pressure to come up with a monetary value. The concern with using talent development staff is their ownership of the program in question increases bias and often results in loss of credibility, especially when reporting a very high ROI.

Let's consider an example of using estimation to convert the measure of absenteeism to monetary value. Say you have an absenteeism problem, you implement a solution, and, as a result, the absenteeism problem is resolved. You now want to place a monetary value on an absence. You have no standard value. You don't want to invest the resources to develop a value using historical costs. There are no internal or external experts who can tell you. You've been unsuccessful in looking for an external database. You have no other measures that have been converted to monetary value to which you can link absenteeism. With pressure to come up with an ROI for this particular program, you decide to go to estimation.

The first step is determining who knows best what happened when an unexpected absence occurred. So, to convert the measure to monetary value, you call in five supervisors from similar work units to discuss the issue and help develop a value for an absence. Using a structured focus group approach, the scenario plays out as follows.

At the beginning of the focus group session, discuss the issue with the five supervisors, explaining why they have been brought together and that you are attempting to place a monetary value on an unexpected absence. Spend a few minutes in conversation about the issue before continuing the process. Then ask Supervisor 1, "What happens when someone does not show up for work?" Supervisor 1 ponders the question for a moment and says, "When someone doesn't show up for work, I have to call in a replacement. I hand the most pressing issues off to another employee who then has to interrupt her work to tend to the urgent tasks of the absent employee." Then go to Supervisors 2, 3, 4, and 5. Each supervisor takes about two minutes to tell what happens when someone doesn't show up for work.

Next have each supervisor estimate the monetary value or what it is costing the organization when unexpected absences and associated events occur. Ask Supervisor 1, "Based on what you have told us about what occurs when someone does not show up for work, how much do you think one absence costs the organization per day?" Supervisor 1 considers her issues and all that occurs around an unexpected absence and says, "Based on what happens in my office when someone doesn't show up for work, I believe it costs us about $1,000 per day per absence." Write it on a flipchart. Ask Supervisor 2 the same question. Supervisor 2 considers what Supervisor 1 said, but then she thinks about her own situation. She responds: "I understand where Supervisor 1 is coming from with her estimate, but given what happens in my department, I believe it costs more. I estimate it costs about $1,500 a day for an unexpected absence." Write it on a flipchart. Ask the same question of Supervisors 3, 4, and 5. Now it's time to adjust for error.

Estimates are subjective; therefore, to reduce the error in the estimate, adjust for the supervisors' confidence. Start with Supervisor 1 saying, "You've explained what happens when someone doesn't show up for work. You estimate that it costs you $1,000 per day per unexpected absence. You've heard what happens in other supervisors' functions and how much they believe it's costing them when someone doesn't show up for work. Now, given what happens in your organization and your estimated costs and what you have heard from others, how confident are you that your estimate is accurate?" After thinking this over, Supervisor 1 says, "Well, it is an estimate, but I know what happens when people don't show up for work and I can be pretty sure what it's costing us from a time perspective. Given that it is an estimate and I'm not totally sure, I'll say that I am 70 percent confident in my estimate."

Write it next to his or her estimate. Repeat the process with Supervisors 2, 3, 4, and 5. Table 5-4 shows the estimates of the five supervisors and their error adjustments. Multiply each estimate by the error adjustment, then total and average the adjusted values. The results are an average adjusted per-day cost for one absence of $1,061.

Figure 5-2 shows what happens when you adjust original estimates by factoring for confidence level. The top line represents the original estimate for each supervisor. The bottom line shows the adjusted value. The additional step to adjust and estimate for error reduces variability in the estimates and provides a more conservative value, hence improving the reliability of the estimated value of one absence.

Table 5-4. Absenteeism Is Converted Using Supervisor Estimates

Supervisor	Estimated Per Day Cost	Percent Confidence	Adjusted Per Day Cost
1	$1,000	70%	$700
2	$1,500	65%	$975
3	$2,300	50%	$1,150
4	$2,000	60%	$1,200
5	$1,600	80%	$1,280
			$5,305
Average adjusted per day cost of one absence			$1,061

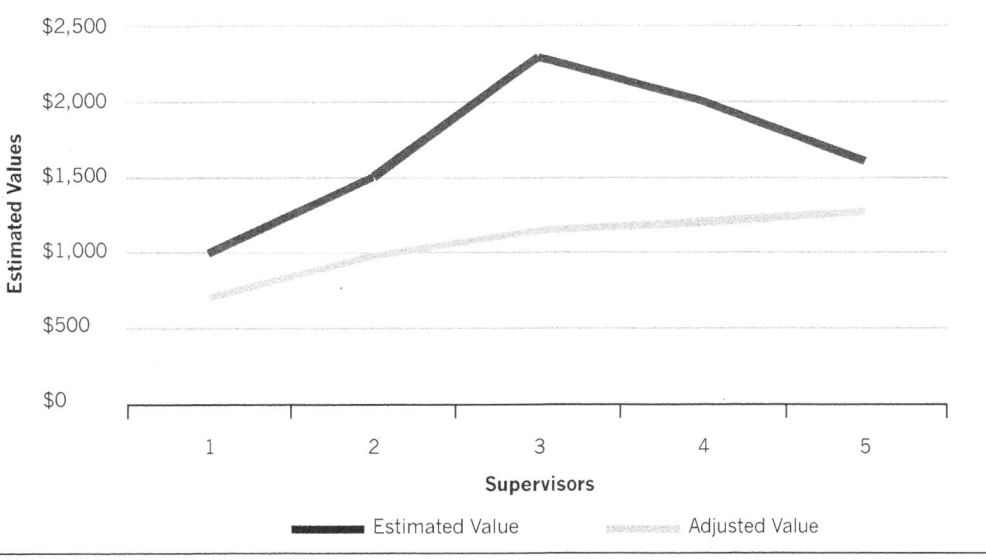

Figure 5-2. Estimated Value of Absenteeism

Data Conversion Four-Part Test

For those times when you cannot decide whether you can credibly convert a measure to monetary value, complete this four-part test:

1. If the measure you want to convert has a standard value, convert it to monetary value.

2. If there is not a standard value, is there a method other than standard values to get there? If there is not a method, then report the measure as intangible.
3. If there is a method to convert the measure, can you do so with minimum resources? If no, then report it as intangible. (You don't want to spend more on data conversion than the evaluation itself.)
4. If you can convert the measure to monetary value using minimum resources, can you convince your executive in two minutes or less that the value is credible? If no, report the measure as intangible. If yes, convert it!

Figure 5-3 presents the four-part test as a flowchart.

Figure 5-3. To Convert or Not to Convert

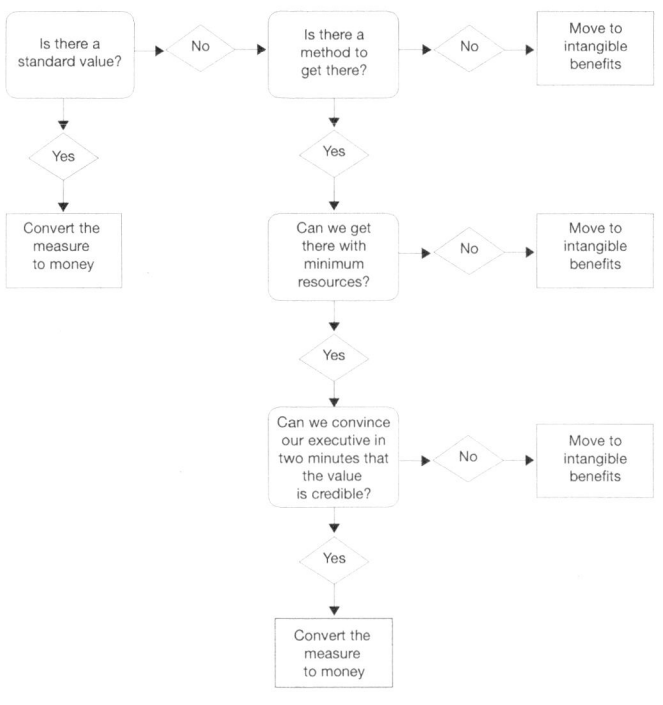

Five Steps to Calculating Monetary Benefits

When you have decided to convert a measure to monetary value and chosen the technique that you're going to use to calculate the monetary value, then you are going to follow five steps to calculate part of the numerator in the ROI formula, or the program benefits:

1. Focus on the unit of measure.
2. Determine the value of each unit.
3. Calculate the change in the performance of the measure.
4. Determine the annual improvement in the measure.
5. Calculate the total monetary value of the improvement.

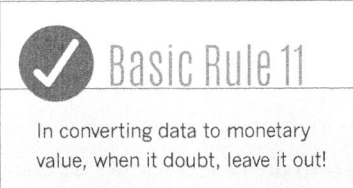

Basic Rule 11

In converting data to monetary value, when it doubt, leave it out!

Focus on the Unit of Measure

The first step is simply reducing the objective to specific units of measure. If you are evaluating a measure of productivity and the output is credit card accounts, the unit of measure is one credit card account.

Determine the Value of Each Unit

In determining the value of each unit, use standard values or one of the other operational techniques. In the credit card account example, you may find that one new account is worth $1,000. This figure is based on standard values using profit contribution. So, the value is $1,000 in profit.

Calculate the Change in the Performance of the Measure

Step 3 is the result of the Level 4 analysis, after isolating the program effects on improvement in the measure. How many new credit card accounts did you open due to the program? Let's assume that on average the bank saw an increase in five new credit card accounts per month.

Determine the Annual Improvement in the Measure.

Annualize the improvement in the measure. Remember that Guiding Principle 9 (from chapter 2) says that for short-term programs you are going to report only first-year benefits. You are not going to wait one year to determine the annual impact. Rather, based on the program objectives, you will pick a point in time to get the average improvement to that date, and then annualize that figure, but only for one year versus multiple years. The first-year-only rule maintains a conservative approach. In the credit card account example, the unit of measure is one account and the value of the measure is $1,000. The change in performance of the measure due to the program (after isolating the program) is five new accounts per month. To determine the annual improvement in the measure, multiply the change in performance by 12 months. So, five per month times 12 months equals 60 new accounts due to the program.

Calculate the Total Monetary Value of the Improvement

Take the number from step 4, annual improvement in the measure (60 in the example) and multiply it by the value of the measure ($1,000 in the example). The total monetary value of improvement is $60,000. This is the value that goes in the numerator of the equation. Table 5-5 shows this calculation step-by-step.

$$\text{BCR} = \frac{\text{Program Benefits (\$60,000)}}{\text{Program Costs}}$$

$$\text{ROI (\%)} = \frac{(\text{Program Benefits [\$60,000]} - \text{Program Costs})}{\text{Program Costs}} \times 100$$

Table 5-5. Five Steps to Program Benefits

1. Focus on the unit of measure.
    1 credit card account
2. Determine the value of each unit.
    $1,000 profit per 1 credit card account per year
3. Calculate the change in the performance of the measure.
    5 new credit card accounts per month (after isolating other variables)
4. Determine the annual improvement in the measure.
    5 accounts per month × 12 months = 60 new credit card accounts per year
5. Calculate the total monetary value of the improvement
    60 per year × $1,000 per account = $60,000 annual value of the improvement

Now, you do it! Exercise 5-1 provides the information for each of the steps. All you have to do is complete steps 4 and 5. The answer to this exercise is found at the end of this chapter.

Calculate ROI

Exercise 5-1. Converting Data to Monetary Values

Scenario: Placing monetary value on grievance reduction		
Step 1	**Focus on the unit of measure** Our unit of measure is 1 grievance.	
Step 2	**Determine the value of each unit** The value of each unit is $6,500, as determined by internal experts.	
Step 3	**Calculate the change in the performance of the measure** The number of grievances declined by 10 per month; and after isolating the effects of the program, 7 of the 10 fewer grievances were due to the program.	
Step 4	**Determine the annual improvement in the measure** The annual change in performance equals _____.	
Step 5	**Calculate the total monetary value of the improvement** The annual change in performance times the value equals _____.	

The value that you put in step 5 is the value that goes in the numerator of the formula.

$$\text{BCR} = \frac{\text{Program Benefits (Value From Step 5)}}{\text{Program Costs}}$$

$$\text{ROI (\%)} = \frac{\text{(Program Benefits [Value From Step 5]} - \text{Program Costs)}}{\text{Program Costs}} \times 100$$

Tabulating Fully Loaded Costs

This next step in the move from Level 4 to Level 5 is tabulating the program costs. The final cost figure will be inserted in the ROI formula twice: first to be subtracted from the final benefits figure to calculate net program benefits; second to be divided into the net program benefits figure. When taking an evaluation to Level 4 only, this step is not necessary; although, regardless of how you evaluate your programs, it should be common practice to know the full costs of the talent development function and its various programs.

What is meant by *fully loaded costs*? It means everything. Table 5-6 shows the four categories of costs. Which do you think make up the full cost of the program?

Chapter 5

Table 5-6. Cost Categories

Which Cost Category Is Appropriate for ROI?	
A	**B**
• Operating costs • Support costs	• Administrative costs • Participant compensation • Facility costs • Classroom costs
C	**D**
• Program development costs • Administrative costs • Classroom costs • Participant costs	• Analysis costs • Development costs • Implementation costs • Delivery costs • Evaluation costs • Overhead and administrative costs

If you selected category D, you are correct. The analysis and the development costs are prorated over the life of the program, so one ROI study will not be weighed down by the full costs of analysis and development. But a fair portion of those costs will be included. The lifetime of the program is considered the time until a major program change occurs. Say you are evaluating a program that will not change for one year and you offer the program 10 times during the year. When you conduct an ROI study on one offering of that program, your analysis costs and your development costs will be included only at the rate of one-tenth of the total of the analysis and development costs. The other offerings are going to benefit from the investment in analysis and development as well. Program materials, instructor and facilitator costs, facilities costs, travel, lodging, meals, participant salary and benefits, and evaluation costs are expensed—they are the direct costs.

Overhead and administrative costs, however, are allocated based on the number of days or hours required of participants to engage in the program. Table 5-7 provides an example. As you see in the table, the unallocated budget in the example is $548,061. To calculate the total number of participant-days, consider the number of days for a program and multiply it by the number of times the program is offered (a five-day program offered 10 times a year equals 50 participant-days). In the example, there are 7,400 participant-days. The next step is to determine the per-day cost of the unallocated budget. The unallocated budget divided by the number of participant-days gives a per-day cost of $74 ($548,061 ÷ 7,400 = $74). The per-day costs are allocated to the number of days involved in the

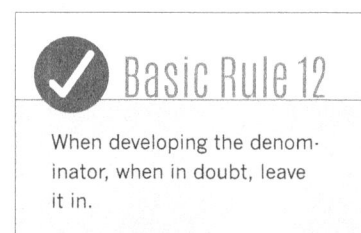

Basic Rule 12

When developing the denominator, when in doubt, leave it in.

program being evaluated. If the program is a three-day training program, you would allocate $222 to overhead and administrative costs.

Table 5-7. Allocation of Overhead and Administrative Costs

Unallocated budget	$548,061
Total number of participant-days *(5-day program offered 10 times a year equals 50 participant days)*	7,400
Per-day unallocated budget *($548,061 ÷ 7,400)*	$74
Overhead and administrative costs allocated to a three-day program *(3 × $74)*	$222

Table 5-8 provides a worksheet to help you develop the fully loaded costs for your talent development programs.

Calculating the ROI

As explained in chapter 1, while there are any number of metrics indicating economic success of an organization and its individual investments, two metrics work with all types of programs: the benefit-cost ratio (BCR) or the ROI percentage. In simple terms, the BCR compares the economic benefits of the program with the cost of the program. A BCR of 2:1 says that for every $1 you invest, you get $2 back in gross benefits.

The ROI formula is reported as a percentage. The ROI is developed by calculating the net program benefits divided by program costs times 100. A BCR of 2:1 translates into an ROI of 100 percent. This tells you that for every $1 you spend you get $1 back, after costs. Remember that you're working with net benefits and the ROI is reported as a percentage. The formula used here is essentially the same as ROI in other types of investments where the standard equation is annual earnings divided by investment.

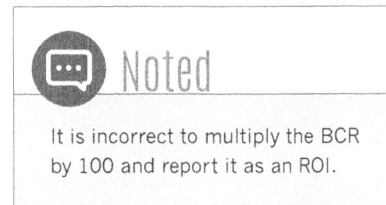

Noted

It is incorrect to multiply the BCR by 100 and report it as an ROI.

Table 5-8. Cost Estimating Worksheet

Analysis Costs	Total
Salaries and employee benefits—talent development staff *(no. of people × average salary × employee benefits factor × no. of hours on project)*	___
Meals, travel, and incidental expenses	___
Office supplies and expenses	___
Printing and reproduction	___
Outside services	___
Equipment expenses	___
Registration fees	___
Other miscellaneous expenses	___
Total Analysis Cost	___

Development Costs	Total
Salaries and employee benefits *(no. of people × avg. salary × employee benefits factor × no. of hours on project)*	___
Meals, travel, and incidental expenses	___
Office supplies and expenses	___
Program materials and supplies	___
Film ___	
Videotape ___	
Audiotapes ___	
Artwork ___	
Manuals and materials ___	
Other ___	
Printing and reproduction	___
Outside services	___
Equipment expense	___
Other miscellaneous expenses	___
Total development costs	___

Delivery Costs	Total
Participant costs	___

Salaries and employee benefits
    *(no. of participants × avg. salary × employee benefits factor ×
    hrs. or days of training time)* ___	

Meals, travel, and accommodations *(no. of participants × avg. daily expenses × days of training)* ___	
Program materials and supplies	___
Participant replacement costs (if applicable)	___
Lost production (explain basis)	___

Instructor costs
    Salaries and benefits
    Meals, travel, and incidental expenses
    Outside services
Facility costs
Facilities rental
Facilities expense allocation
Equipment expenses
Other miscellaneous expenses

Total delivery costs

Evaluation Costs   Total

Salaries and employee benefits—talent development staff
(no. of people × avg. salary × employee benefits factor × no. of hours on project)
Meals, travel, and incidental expenses
Participant costs
Office supplies and expenses
Printing and reproduction
Outside services
Equipment expenses
Other miscellaneous expenses

Total evaluation costs

General Overhead Allocation

Total program costs

W

Remember that intangible benefits are those that you choose not to convert to monetary value. But they are sometimes more important than the actual ROI calculation. Typical intangible benefits that you do not convert to monetary value are job satisfaction, organizational commitment, teamwork, and customer satisfaction. You can convert these measures to monetary value; typically, however, when job satisfaction, organizational commitment, teamwork, and customer satisfaction are improved, you're satisfied enough with the improvement in these measures that the dollar value with that improvement is not relevant.

Getting It Done

You have completed almost all the steps in the ROI Methodology. Now, it's time to complete the next three columns in the ROI analysis plan. In chapter 4, you transferred your Level 4 measures to the ROI analysis plan; you selected techniques to isolate the effects of the program on the measure. Now, determine how you will convert these measures to monetary value. If your measure does not pass the four-part test explained earlier, move the measure to the intangible benefits column. Identify the program costs that you plan to consider and those benefits that you plan to categorize as intangibles.

In the next chapter, you will read about the final phase in the ROI Methodology: Optimize Results. This phase requires that you communicate results to key stakeholders and use black box thinking to drive an increase in your talent development funding.

Answers to Exercise 5-1. Converting Data to Monetary Values

Scenario: Placing monetary value on grievance reduction

Step 1 Focus on the unit of measure
Our unit of measure is 1 grievance.

Step 2 Determine the value of each unit
The value of each unit is $6,500, as determined by internal experts.

Step 3 Calculate the change in the performance of the measure
The number of grievances declined by 10 per month; and after isolating the effects of the program, 7 of the 10 fewer grievances were due to the program.

Step 4 Determine the annual improvement in the measure
The annual change in performance equals **84.**

Step 5 Calculate the total monetary value of the improvement
The annual change in performance times the value equals **$546,000.**

The value that you put in step 5 is the value that goes in the numerator of the formula.

$$BCR = \frac{\text{Program Benefits (\$546,000)}}{\text{Program Costs}}$$

$$ROI\,(\%) = \frac{(\text{Program Benefits [\$546,000]} - \text{Program Costs})}{\text{Program Costs}} \times 100$$

6

Optimize Results

What's Inside This Chapter

The chapter describes the basics of the last phase in the ROI Methodology: Optimize results. Specifically, this chapter covers:

- telling the story
- developing reports
- using black box thinking.

6

Optimize Results

Telling the Story

Measurement and evaluation are meaningless endeavors if the results of the evaluation are not communicated in such a way that compels your audience to take action. It is through action that the ultimate purpose of measurement and evaluation can be achieved. That purpose? To drive improvement in organizational measures that matter.

Interestingly, communicating results and storytelling are among the skill gaps most often cited when assessing analytics capabilities. A 2018 Institute for Corporate Productivity (i4cp)/ROI Institute research study titled *Four Ways to Advance Your People Analytics Practice* showed that a competency most important to (but lacking in the people analytics practice) is storytelling, which is tied for second place with qualitative methodologies. Only quantitative analysis was more important. Figure 6-1 summarizes the findings of this survey question.

The gap in such skills has not gone unnoticed by conference providers and publishers. Today, more than ever in the past, conference agendas are filled with various approaches to get the word out. Publishers are embracing the topic by producing a variety of content and books on the topic. Technology providers are working overtime trying to one-up each other on the best way to display data so that the pertinent versus merely relevant information are accessible to audiences. On top of the need for storytelling is the need to nudge audiences to act on the data—in other words, optimizing information to improve programs and processes.

Communication, as with programs, must be designed to achieve results. This requires understanding the context in which the communication will occur; defining audiences, modes, modalities, and techniques that will enable and encourage the audience to listen and act; delivering the communication in a compelling and logical way; and evaluating the communication to ensure it is effective. So, just like a talent development program, communication and storytelling are designed to deliver insight and information that people will and can act on to achieve an outcome.

Figure 6-1. People Analytics Competencies That Are Important But Lacking

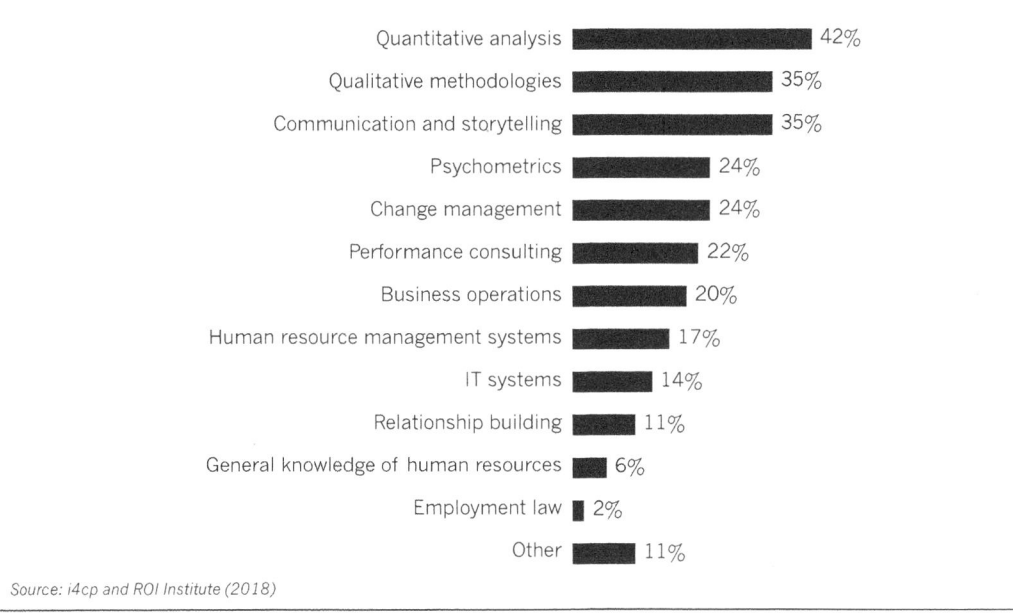

Source: i4cp and ROI Institute (2018)

A basic approach to design the communication of your evaluation findings is to consider three questions:

- What do you need?
- Who can give it to you?
- How do you ask for it?

What Do You Need?

Good communication can address a variety of needs. Needs range from getting approval for your programs to satisfying curiosity about the talent development function. Sometimes you are looking for additional support and affirmation for your efforts or for agreement that a change in a program needs to occur. Other times you just want credibility for your programs, thereby reporting results of your study to the general audience. Often you want to reinforce the need to make changes to the system to further support the transfer of learning. Or you communicate results of your evaluations to prepare the talent development staff for changes in the organization or, better yet, to apprise the staff of opportunities to help them develop their skills.

Communication is often conducted to enhance the entire process and to emphasize a specific program's importance to the organization. The communication process is used to explain what is going on, why something might or might not have occurred, and what the goals are to improve a program when it results in a negative ROI. You can use the communication process to energize the talent development staff as well as senior management and supervisors about an upcoming program. Finally, you can demonstrate how tools, skills, or new knowledge can be applied to the organization.

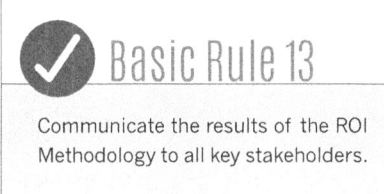

Basic Rule 13

Communicate the results of the ROI Methodology to all key stakeholders.

When a pilot program shows impressive results, use this opportunity to stimulate interest among stakeholders in continuing the program—and interest for employees to participate in it. Table 6-1 provides a list of possible purposes to consider in determining why you want to communicate the process and the results.

Table 6-1. Checklist of Needs for Communicating Results

1. **Needs Related to Talent Development Programs**
   - ❏ Demonstrate accountability for client expenditures.
   - ❏ Secure approval for a program.
   - ❏ Gain support for all programs.
   - ❏ Enhance reinforcement of the program.
   - ❏ Enhance the results of future programs.
   - ❏ Show complete results of the program.
   - ❏ Explain a program's negative ROI.
   - ❏ Seek agreement for changes to a program.
   - ❏ Stimulate interest in upcoming programs.
   - ❏ Encourage participation in programs.
   - ❏ Market future programs.

2. **Needs Related to Talent Development Staff**
   - ❏ Build credibility for the staff.
   - ❏ Prepare the staff for changes.
   - ❏ Provide opportunities for staff to develop skills.

3. **Needs Related to the Organization at Large**
   - ❏ Reinforce the need for system changes to support learning transfer.
   - ❏ Demonstrate how tools, skills, and knowledge add value to the organization.
   - ❏ Explain current processes.

Who Can Give It to You?

Once you identify your needs, the next step is to target the message to the audience who can best give you what you need. If you are communicating results so that you can secure approval for a new program, consider your client or the top executive your target audience. If you are trying to gain support for a program, consider the immediate managers or team leaders of the targeted participant group. If you are interested in improving the immediate talent development process, including facilitation as well as the learning environment, target the talent development staff. If you want to demonstrate accountability for all talent development programs, target all employees in the organization. It is important to think through who can help you address and respond to your communication need. Some key questions that you want to ask when determining the most appropriate audience are:

- Is the potential audience interested in the program?
- Does the potential audience really want to or need to receive this information?
- Has someone already made a commitment to this audience regarding communication?
- Is the timing right for this message to be presented to this audience?
- Is the potential audience familiar with the program?
- How does this audience prefer to have results communicated to them?
- Is the audience likely to find the results threatening?
- Which medium will be most convenient to the audience?

There are four primary audiences to whom you will always communicate the results of your ROI studies: the talent development team, participants, participants' supervisors, and clients.

Talent Development Team

The talent development team should receive constant communication of the results of all levels of evaluation. Levels 1 and 2 data should be reported to the talent development team immediately after the program. This provides them the opportunity to adjust the program prior to the next offering. It also provides them information to consider when developing their professional development plan. Results at Levels 3, 4, and 5 should be communicated as soon as they become available. The team is accountable for ensuring program design delivers on its promises; so, they should be the first to know whether it did.

Participants

Participants are a critical source of data. Without participants, there are no data. Levels 1 and 2 data should be reported back to participants immediately after the data have been analyzed. A summary copy of the final ROI study should also be provided to participants. In doing so, participants see that the data that they are providing to you is actually being used to make improvements to the program. This enhances the potential for additional and even better data in future evaluations.

One caveat is when the Level 4: Impact results and the Level 5: ROI metric could lead to negative response from participants. If this is the situation, then manage this communication with extra care. While the impact and ROI results are important to those funding the program and processes, they may sometimes communicate the wrong message to participants and other employees. Also, following up with participants after you have adjusted a program reinforces that what participants tell you is important to the success of the program and contributes value to the organization as a whole.

Participants' Supervisors

Your participants' supervisors are critical to a program's success. Without supervisor support for a program, participants will struggle to engage, which jeopardizes the successful transfer of learning on the job when participants return to work. By reporting the ROI study results to supervisors, you will clearly demonstrate to them that employee participation in programs yields performance improvement. Supervisors will see the importance of their own roles in supporting the learning process from program attendance to application.

Think About This

Just like there are guiding principles to the ROI Methodology, there are principles for communicating the results of an ROI study. The following list provides a broad view of these principles:
- Keep communication timely.
- Target communication to specific audiences.
- Carefully select communication media.
- Keep communication consistent with past practices.
- Incorporate testimonials from influential individuals.
- Consider the talent development function's reputation when developing the overall strategy.

Clients

The fourth group to whom you should always communicate the results of your ROI study is the client, the person or persons who fund the program. Here, it is important to report the full scope of success. The client wants to see the program impact on the business as well as the actual ROI. Although Levels 1 and 2 data are only marginally important to the client to some extent, it is unnecessary to report this data to the client immediately after the program. The client's greatest interest is in Levels 4 and 5 data. Providing the client a summary report for the comprehensive evaluations will ensure that the client sees that programs are successful and, in the event of an unsuccessful program, that a plan is in place to take corrective action.

How Do You Ask?

Consider the best means for asking for what you need. As in other steps in the ROI Methodology, you have many options to communicate information—meetings, internal publications, electronic media, program brochures, case studies, and formal reports. Your choice of communication medium is important, especially in the early stages of implementing the ROI Methodology. You want to make sure that you select the appropriate medium for the particular communication need and target audience.

Meetings

When considering meetings as the medium for telling your story, you have several criteria to take into account. First, organizations are swamped with endless meetings. It helps to review when regularly scheduled meetings occur and plan for communication during them so you are not disrupting your audiences' schedules. However, you do run the risk of having to wait to present your report until a future meeting when you can be added to the agenda. Key players might be so interested in your ROI study that they won't mind you scheduling the earliest possible meeting.

If it's not a staff or management meeting, you might schedule a discussion where you, a participant, and maybe a participant's supervisor create a panel to discuss a particular program. Panel discussions can also occur at regularly scheduled meetings or at a special meeting focused on the program.

Business update meetings also present opportunities to provide information about your program. Best practice meetings, where each function within an organization shares results, are another opportunity to present the results of your programs. Or you might present your ROI study at a large conference in a panel discussion, which includes talent development professionals and managers from a variety of organizations.

Internal Publications

Internal publications are another way in which you can communicate to the employees. You can use these internal publications—newsletters, memos, breakroom bulletin boards—to report program progress and results as well as to generate interest in current and future programs. Internal hard copy communications are the perfect opportunity to recognize program participants who have provided data or responded promptly to your questionnaires. If you have offered incentives for participation in a program or for prompt responses to questionnaires, mention this in these publications. Use internal publications to tell human interest stories and highlight activities, actions, and encounters that occur during and as a result of the program. Be sure to accentuate the positive and announce compliments and congratulations generously.

Electronic Media

Digitization is leading to new types of electronic media that support the dissemination of information. Websites, intranets, and group emailing tend to remain foundational approaches, and are often used to promote programs and processes being implemented in the organization. While social media platforms are useful, one would never disseminate the details of an ROI study through such means. However, they can be useful for sharing snippets of information that promote program success or even changes that resulted from your study. Take advantage of these opportunities to spread the word about the activities and successes of the talent development department.

Brochures

Program brochures are another way to promote talent development activities and offerings. Reporting results in a brochure that describes the program's process and highlights the program's successes can generate interest in your current program, stimulate interest in coming programs, and enhance respect and regard for the talent development function and staff.

While some would argue that brochures have become obsolete in today's world of digital communication, digital and paper-based brochures remain important communication tools, particularly when marketing successful programs to internal and external audiences.

Formal Reports

A final medium through which to report results is in the formal report. There are two types of reports—micro-level reports and macro-level scorecards—that are used to tell the success of talent development programs. Micro-level reports present the results of a specific program and include detailed reports, executive summaries, general audience reports, and single-page reports. Macro-level scorecards are an important tool in reporting the overall success of the talent development function. In the next section, we dive deeper into developing these reports.

Developing Reports

There are five types of reports to develop to communicate the results of the ROI studies. These include detailed reports, which are developed for every evaluation project; executive summaries; general audience reports; single-page reports; and macro-level scorecard.

Detailed Reports

The detailed report is the comprehensive report that details the specifics of the program and the ROI study. This report is developed for every comprehensive evaluation that you conduct. It becomes your record and allows you the opportunity to replicate the study without having to repeat the entire planning process. By building on an existing study, you can save time, money, effort, and a great deal of frustration. The detailed report contains six major headings: need for the program, need for the evaluation, evaluation methodology, results, conclusions and next steps, and appendixes.

Need for the Program

In this part of the report, you define and clarify the objectives for the program, making sure that the objectives reflect the five levels of evaluation. You should have objectives that relate to participant perspective, describe what participants are intended to learn, reflect how participants are intended to apply what they have learned, and reflect the outcomes that the knowledge and skills gained in this program will have on the organization. You will also present your target ROI and how you came to that target.

Need for the Evaluation

Typically, if the program is intended to influence Level 4: Impact measures, this presents a need for evaluation. But, in some cases, it may be that the Level 4 measures were never developed so the intent of the evaluation is to understand the influence the program has had or is having on the organization. The intent of the evaluation may be to understand the extent to which the program successfully achieved the objectives. Or, the need for the evaluation may depend on the request of an executive. Clearly state the reasons in the report. Again, although this report will be distributed to key audiences, it is also the report that serves as the tool to refer to in future evaluations and to remind you what happened during this evaluation.

Evaluation Methodology

This clear, concise, and complete description of the evaluation process builds credibility for the results. It also supports replication for future evaluations. Provide an overview of the evaluation approach. Then describe each element of the process, including all options available at each step, which options you chose, the reasons for your choice, all actions and activities related to each element of the process, and each step you took. For the data collection section of the report, spell out how you collected the data, why you collected that data, from whom you collected the data, why you collected the data from that source, when you collected the data, and why you settled on the data collection procedures that you did. Display a complete copy in detail of your data collection plan. Then, explain the ROI analysis procedures. Here, you will set out why you chose the method you used to isolate the effects of the program. Clearly state the ways in which you isolated the effects of the program. With regards to data conversion, explain how you developed the monetary values for the Level 4: Impact measures linked to the program, again setting out the range of possibilities for data conversion. List the different ways and explain why you chose the techniques you chose. Address the cost issue and provide the cost categories that you included in your ROI analysis. A word of caution: At this point, refrain from including the actual program costs. Bear in mind that if you present the cost of the program to your audience too early, they will focus on the cost of the program and you will lose their attention. As with data collection, provide a detailed copy of the ROI analysis plan so that your audience can see a summary of exactly what you did.

Results

Now, it's time for your story—the results section, where the talent development program that has undergone this rigorous evaluation can shine! Here, you will provide the results for all levels of evaluation beginning with Level 1: Reaction and Planned Action. Explain the intent for gathering reaction data, providing the specific questions the reaction data answer, and report the results. Move from there to Level 2: Learning. Explain why it is important to evaluate learning and the key questions that learning data answer followed by the results. Present next the Level 3: Application and Implementation results. Here, provide evidence that what was taught was used. Talk about how effectively knowledge and skills gained in the program have been applied by the participants and how frequently they have applied their new knowledge and skills. Discuss how the support system enabled participants to apply what they learned. Present barriers to the transfer of learning and how they might be overcome in the future. Explain that when you realized, through the evaluation process, that a problem was occurring and that the support system was not helping, you took action by going to talk to those who might know or who might provide information about how things could be changed to support the program next time.

Next, present Level 4: Impact results, including how the program positively influenced specific organizational outcomes. Here again, reinforce the fact that you isolated the effects of the program to ensure you controlled for other factors that might have contributed to these outcomes. Describe your options for isolation and explain why you chose the option you chose.

Now report on Level 5: ROI. First, explain what is meant by ROI, clearly defining the ROI formula. Address the benefits of the program, the Level 4 measures, and how you achieved them. Explain how you converted data to monetary value; detail the monetary benefits of the program. Then, report the fully loaded costs of the program. Recall that earlier in the evaluation methodology section of the report you described the details of the cost items but did not provide the dollar value. It is here, after monetary benefits are reported, where you set out the dollar values of the costs. The readers have already seen the benefits in dollar amounts; now give them the costs. If the benefits exceed the costs, then the pain of a very expensive program is relieved because the audience can clearly see that the benefits outweigh the costs. Finally, provide the ROI calculation.

The last part of the results section in the detailed report concerns intangible benefits. As you've learned throughout the book, intangible benefits are those items you choose not to convert to monetary value. Highlight those intangible benefits and the unplanned benefits that came about through the program. Reinforce their importance and the value they represent.

Basic Rule 14

Hold reporting the actual ROI until the end of the results section.

Conclusions and Next Steps

Develop and report your conclusions based on the evaluation, answering these questions:
- Was the program successful?
- What needs to be improved?
- How best should the organization address improvement opportunities?

Explain the next steps, clearly pointing out the next actions to be taken with this program. Those actions could include continuing the program, adding new content, removing content, developing new job aids, converting some components from instructor-led facilitation to e-learning format, or developing a blended learning approach to reduce the training costs while maintaining the benefits you achieved from the program. Clearly identify the next steps and set out the dates by which these steps will be completed.

Appendixes

The appendixes include exhibits, detailed tables that could not feasibly be included in the text, and raw data (keeping the data items confidential). Again, the final report is a reference for you as well as a story of success for others.

Throughout your report, incorporate quotes—positive and negative—from respondents. Remember that there are ethical issues with evaluation. It might be tempting to leave out negative comments; however, you will enhance your credibility and gain respect for the talent development function if you tell the story as it is. By developing this detailed comprehensive report, you will have backup for anything that you say during a presentation. When conducting a future ROI study on a similar program, you will have your road map in front of you. Table 6-2 presents a sample outline of a detailed report.

Table 6-2. Detailed Report Outline

Detailed Report Outline Entry	Purpose
General Information • Objectives of Study • Background	
Methodology for Impact Study • Levels of Evaluation • ROI Process • Collecting Data • Isolating the Effects of Training • Converting Data to Monetary Values • Costs **Assumptions (Guiding Principles)**	Builds credibility for the process.
Results • General Information 　» Response Profile 　» Relevance of Materials • Participant Reaction • Learning • Application and Implementation 　» Success With Use 　» Barriers 　» Enables • Impact 　» General Comments 　» Linkage With Business Measures • ROI • Intangible Benefits	The results with six measures: Levels 1, 2, 3, 4, 5, and intangibles
Conclusions and Recommendations • Conclusions • Recommendations	
Appendix	

Executive Summaries

Another important report to develop is the executive summary. The executive summary follows the same outline as the detailed report although you exclude the appendixes and do not develop each section and subsection in detail. You will clearly and concisely explain the need for the program, the need for the evaluation, and the evaluation methodology. Always include the methodology prior to the results. Why? When the reader understands and appreciates the methodology, they typically have a greater appreciation for the results. Report the data from Level 1 through Level 5 and include the sixth measure of success—the intangible benefits. The executive summary is usually 10 to 15 pages in length.

General Audience Reports

General audience reports are a great way to describe the success of your programs to the employees. General audience reports may be published in organization publications, like newsletters or in-house magazines; reported in management and team meetings, where you briefly review the report in a meeting setting; and, finally, published as case studies. Case studies can be published internally and externally. There are many opportunities to publish your story outside your organization, including trade or association publications or academic research publications. The key here is to tell the story to show that your programs are working and that, when they don't work, you are willing to take steps to improve the program.

Single-Page Reports

A final micro-level report is a single-page report or micro-level dashboard that summarizes the results. Table 6-3 shows an example of a single-page report. Figure 6-2 shows a dashboard from Explorance's Metrics That Matter (MTM) system. Single-page reports are used with great care. Reporting success of your program using the single-page report or micro-level dashboard can be risky if your audience is unfamiliar with the process. If an audience sees the ROI of a program without having an appreciation for the methodology, members will fixate on the ROI and never notice, much less form a regard for, the information developed in the other levels of evaluation. While these simple micro-level summaries of results have risks, they are an easy way to communicate results to the appropriate audiences on a routine basis.

Table 6-3. Single-Page Report

Sexual Harassment Prevention Program

Level 1: Reaction and Planned Action—Results
- Overall rating of 4.11 out of a possible 5
- 93% provided list of action items

Level 2: Learning—Results
- Post-test scores average 84
- Pretest scores average 51
- Improvement 65%
- Participants demonstrated they could use skills successfully

Level 3: Application and Implementation—Results
- Survey distributed to a sample of 25% of participants (1,720)
- Response rate of 64% (1,102 returned)
  - » 96% conducted meetings with employees and completed meeting record
  - » On a survey of nonsupervisory employees, significant behavior change was noted (4.1 out of 5 scale)
  - » 68% of participants report that all action items were completed
  - » 92% reported that some action items were completed

Level 4: Impact—Results

Sexual Harassment Business Performance Measures	One Year Prior to Program	One Year After Program	Factor for Isolating the Effects of Program
Internal complaints	55	35	74%
External charges	24	14	62%
Litigated complaints	10	6	51%
Legal fees and expenses	$632,000	$481,000	
Settlement/losses	$450,000	$125,000	
Total cost of sexual harassment prevention, investigation, and defense	$1,655,000	$852,000	
Turnover (nonsupervisory annualized)	24.2%	19.9%	

Level 5: ROI—Results
- Total annual benefits $3,200,908
- Total costs $277,987
- ROI   1,052%

Intangible Benefits
- Increased job satisfaction
- Increased teamwork
- Reduced stress

Optimize Results

Figure 6-2. Micro-Level Dashboard

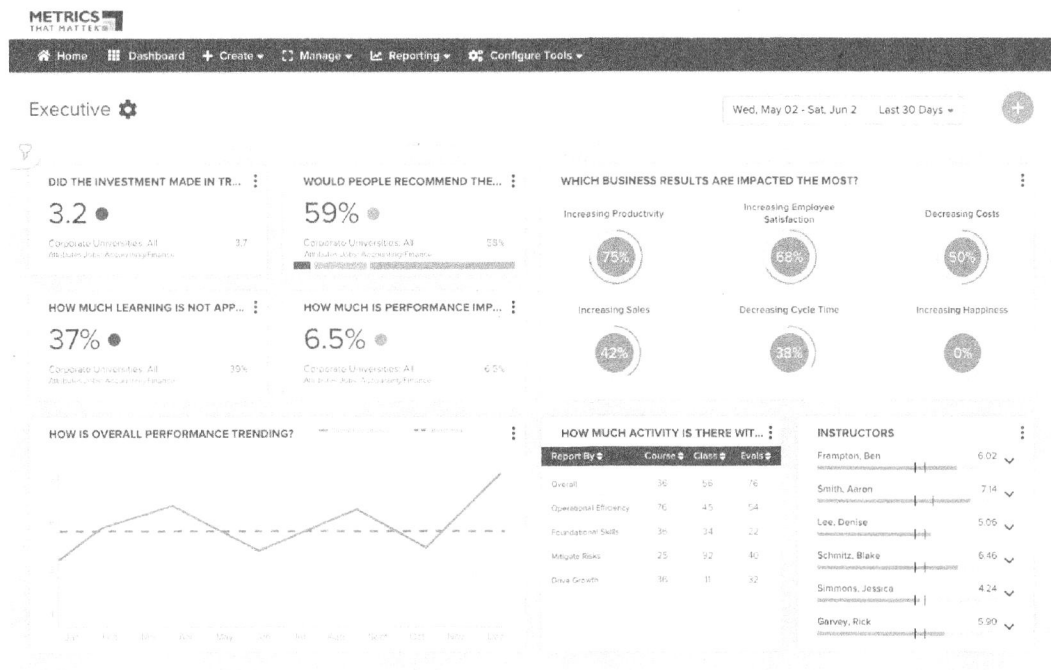

Source: Explorance's Metrics That Matter. Used with permission.

Macro-Level Scorecard

Macro-level scorecards can provide the results of the overall training process. These scorecards provide a macro-level perspective of success and serve as a brief description of program evaluation as contrasted to the detailed report. They show the connection between talent development's contribution and organizational objectives. Methods of isolation are always included in the report to reinforce that you are taking steps to give credit where credit is due. The scorecard integrates a variety of types of data and demonstrates alignment among programs, strategic objectives, and operational goals. Table 6-4 presents an outline of a macro-level scorecard.

Table 6-4. Macro-Level Scorecard Outline

Seven Categories of Data	Entry
Indicators	• Number of employees involved • Total hours of involvement • Hours per employee • Training investment as a percentage of payroll • Cost per participant
Level 1: Reaction and Planned Action	• Percentage of programs evaluated at this level • Ratings on seven items vs. targets • Percentage with action plans • Percentage with ROI forecast
Level 2: Learning	• Percentage of programs evaluated at this level • Types of measurements • Self-assessment ratings on three items vs. targets • Pre/post—average differences
Level 3: Application and Implementation	• Percentage of programs evaluated at this level • Ratings on three items vs. targets • Percentage of action plans completed • Barriers (list of top 10) • Enablers (list of top 10) • Management support profile
Level 4: Impact	• Percent of programs evaluated at this level • Linkage with business measures (list of top 10) • Types of measurement techniques • Types of methods to isolate the effects of programs • Investment perception
Level 5: ROI	• Percentage of programs evaluated at this level • ROI summary for each study • Methods of converting data to monetary value • Fully loaded cost per participant
Intangible Benefits	• Intangibles (list of top 10) • How intangibles were captured

For another example, consider the operations report developed by the Center for Talent Reporting (CTR), a not-for-profit organization. CTR's mission is to develop and promote the adoption of reporting standards for human capital that meet the needs of senior executives, talent management leaders, program managers, and other stakeholders (Figure 6-3). This type of macro-level reporting positions talent development reporting in the same category as other operations reports. It can be an effective way to communicate the success of talent development investments.

Optimize Results

Figure 6-3. Example of a Talent Development Operations Report

			For 2016				
Effectiveness Measures	Unit of Measure	2015 Actual	Plan	June YTD	Comparison to Plan	Forecast	Comparison to Plan
Level 1: Participant Feedback (all programs)							
Quality of content	% favorable	76%	80%	79%	1% below	79%	1% below
Quality of instructor	% favorable	80%	85%	86%	1% above	85%	on plan
Relevance	% favorable	72%	78%	73%	5% below	75%	3% below
Alignment to goals	% favorable	68%	75%	69%	6% below	71%	4% below
Total for Level 1	Average of measures	74%	80%	77%	3% below	78%	2% below
Level 1: Sponsor Feedback (select programs)	% favorable	66%	80%	68%	12% below	75%	5% below
Level 2: Learning (select programs)	Score	78%	85%	83%	2% below	85%	on plan
Level 3: Application rate (select programs)							
Intent to apply (from survey at end of course)	% top two boxes	70%	75%	70%	5% below	72%	3% below
Actual application (after 3 months)	% who applied it	51%	65%	55%	10% below	63%	2% below
Level 4: Impact (select programs)							
Estimate by participants (end of course)	% contribution to goal	20%	25%	15%	10% below	20%	5% below
Level 5: ROI (select programs)							
Net benefits	Thousands $	$546	$800	$250	31%	$650	81%
ROI	%	29%	35%	25%	10% below	30%	5% below

Source: Center for Talent Reporting (www.centerfortalentreporting.org)

 Think About This

There are fundamental guidelines in reporting the results of an ROI results study to senior management. Two critical questions to consider prior to communicating with senior management are whether you will be believed if you have an extremely high ROI and whether senior managers can handle it if you have a negative ROI.

With those two questions in mind, you need to consider the following guidelines:

- Plan a face-to-face meeting with senior managers (first one or two ROI studies).
- Hold results until the end of the presentation.
- Present the complete and balanced sets of measures beginning with Level 1.
- Emphasize the attributes of the methodology that ensure conservative results.
- Present a plan for program improvement.

For the first one or two ROI studies, present your detailed report during a regularly scheduled executive staff meeting. If senior executives know that you have an ROI study to present, they will make room for you on the agenda. Ask for one hour of their time. Present the study in full detail. Have a copy of the comprehensive report for each senior manager available at the meeting. When you begin your presentation, be ready and have copies of your detailed report, but don't give it out before your presentation. If you give them the report, they will be flipping through the pages to find the ROI calculation. Keep the reports beside you as you present your results.

Present the results to the senior management team just as you have written the report: need for program, need for evaluation, evaluation methodology, results, conclusion, and next steps. Be thorough in reporting Levels

149

Chapter 6

1 through 4, and do not fixate on or hurry to the ROI calculation—the entire chain of impact is important to reporting the success of the programs. Report Level 5: ROI and the intangible benefits. Then, present your conclusions and next steps. At the end of your presentation, provide each senior manager a copy of your final report.

Do you really expect the senior management team to read this detailed report? No. At best, they will hand it off to someone else to read and summarize the contents that you will have presented in the meeting. Why then go to the trouble of preparing this printed copy of the detailed final report for senior managers? To build trust. You've told them your story; now, all they have to do is look in the report to see that you covered the details and that you provided a thorough and accurate presentation of the report's contents.

After the first one or two studies, senior management will have bought into the ROI Methodology. Of course, if you've worked the process well, they will have begun to learn the methodology long before your initial presentation. Given that, after the first or second study, you can start distributing the executive summary. Limit your report to senior management to the 10 to 15-page report. Again, it has all the components, but not so many details.

After about five ROI studies, you can begin reporting to senior management using the single-page report, dashboard, scorecard, or even infographic. This will save time and money. Do remember, the talent development staff will always have a copy of the detailed, comprehensive report. This will serve as a backup and a blueprint for future studies.

Data Visualization

Data can be displayed in a variety of ways; the more comprehensive the display of data, the better the story is told within a limited space. Edward R. Tufte is one of the predominant leaders on the topic of graphical display of data. Tufte (1983) suggests that graphical displays of data should:

- Show data.
- Induce the audience to think about the substance rather than the technology of the graphic production.
- Avoid distorting the story that the data have to tell.
- Present many numbers in a small space.
- Make large data sets coherent.
- Encourage the eye to compare different pieces of data.
- Reveal the data at several layers of detail from broad overview to fine structure.
- Serve a reasonably clear purpose: description, exploration, tabulation, or decoration.
- Be closely integrated with the statistical and verbal descriptions of a data set.

A general rule of Tufte's is to show many variables of data in one display. However, it is more important to understand the display and be able to clearly explain the contents of the display rather than provide a comprehensive depiction of your data, but stumble through the story.

In the rest of this section, we'll cover tables, diagrams, and graphs.

Optimize Results

Tables

Tables, sometimes referred to as matrices, are charts that have information arranged in rows and columns. They are simple to explain, are great for summarizing data, and provide one of the best ways to display numerical values. They assist the audience in understanding how the data are organized. They are also one of the most convenient ways of sorting and summarizing data for quick reference.

Only use visual displays of data if it makes the information more accessible and better nudges the audience toward action.

A basic table is shown in Table 6-5. This simple frequency table shows the scores received on an exam in a four-week course. The first column represents the scores; the second column represents the frequency or the number of participants who achieved that score; the third column represents the percent of the total number of participants with that particular score. The valid percent column (sometimes referred to as the adjusted percentage) is based on missing data (scores). In this example, there are no missing scores. So, the valid percent and the percent columns are the same. The cumulative percent column shows the percentage of students who received a certain score or less. For example, 72 percent of the participants scored 88 or less.

Table 6-5. Frequency and Percentage Table

Test Scores	Frequency	Percent[1]	Valid Percent[1]	Cumulative Percent
70	2	11.1	11.1	11.1
77	2	11.1	11.1	22.2
82	1	5.6	5.6	27.8
85	5	27.8	27.8	55.6
87	1	5.6	5.6	61.1
88	2	11.1	11.1	72.2
90	1	5.6	5.6	77.8
92	1	5.6	5.6	83.3
93	2	11.1	11.1	94.4
95	1	5.6	5.6	100.0
Total	18	100	100	

1. Percentages exceed 100 percent.

Table 6-6 is a one-way table that shows two variables along the same axis. This means that two different variables are represented in columns. In the first column is variable 1, which is the participant's name. Variable 2 represents employment dates. This type is most often used in summarizing data from evaluations.

Table 6-6. One-Way Table

Variable 1 ↓	Variable 2 ↓
Participant Name	**Employment Date**
Andrea Adams	November 4, 2015
Benjamin Johnson	January 26, 2019
Robert Ladnier	August 19, 2014
Aisha Mizner	March 15, 2011
Joannetta Ramsey	June 23, 2018

Diagrams

Diagrams are charts made up primarily of geometric shapes, such as circles, rectangles, and triangles, connected by lines or arrows. They show how people, ideas, and things relate. Text is frequently included inside and outside these shapes to tell the story. Numerical values are sometimes used, though to a lesser extent, because diagrams generally display nonquantitative data. Flowcharts, critical path method charts, organization charts, network charts, decision charts, and conceptual charts are frequently presented in diagrams. The four-part test shown as a flowchart in Figure 5-3 is an example of a diagram. Use diagrams to present project timelines, as well as the conceptual framework displaying the findings in an evaluation. Figure 6-4 represents a diagram displaying a phased approach to implementing a full-blown evaluation.

Figure 6-5 is another diagram displaying the argument for the conceptual framework discovered through the evaluation process. In this diagram, the course leads to positive reaction, knowledge acquisition, and the use of knowledge and skills. As a result, there is positive impact on network security, work stoppage, equipment downtime, uptime, and costs of troubleshooting. Through the isolation process, note the other variables that contribute to the Level 4 outcomes. Continuous learning and practice, research, real-world exercises, knowledge application, and reliable staff are listed and graphically depicted as influences on the outcomes. Providing a pictorial framework summarizes the results of the evaluation study in a manner that supports audience understanding.

Figure 6-4. A Phased Approach to a Comprehensive Evaluation

Figure 6-5. Depiction of Conceptual Framework

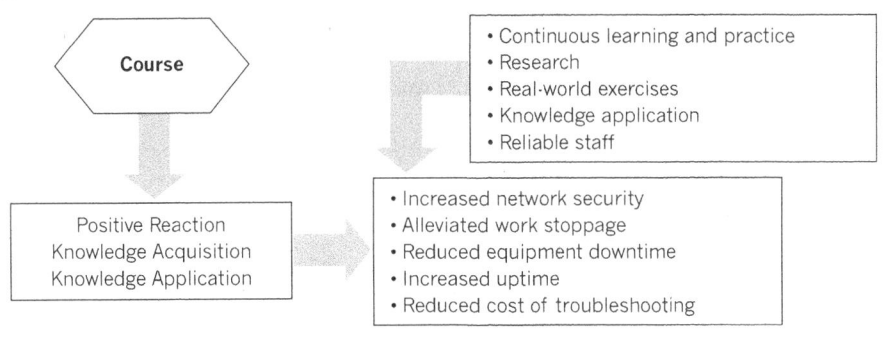

As participants react positively to the course, acquire knowledge and skills, and apply knowledge and skills, results occur. However, other intervening variables also influence measures; therefore, steps must be taken to isolate the effects of the course on these measures.

While diagrams often demonstrate the relationship between quantitative variables, they can also show relationships that are not quantitative in nature. For instance, an organization and social network analysis results in a graphical display of the connections between people as shown in Figure 6-6, where people are represented as circles and their relationships are represented as lines connecting them. This type of graph is a good way to demonstrate the value and use of building new relationships as a result of talent development programs.

Chapter 6

Figure 6-6. Social Network Analysis

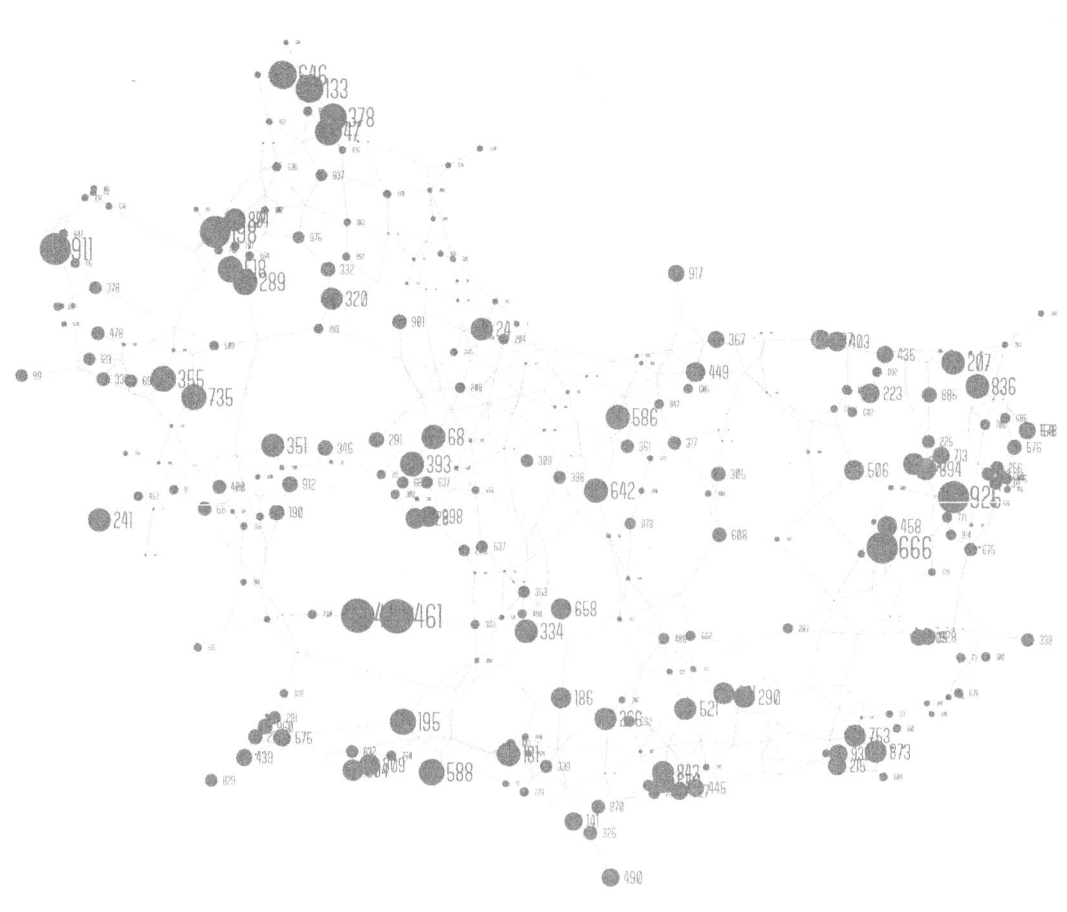

Graphs
Graphs are the most commonly used displays of quantitative relationships between two or more data types. Some types of graphs include bar charts, area graphs, line graphs, scatter graphs, histograms, box plots, and pie charts.

Optimize Results

Histograms

A histogram shows the frequency distribution of the data. As you see in the example in Figure 6-7, the scores of an exam taken by 60 participants in a training program are displayed. The mean score is 72.1 and the standard deviation is 12.0, which tells you that there was a wide variability among the scores. The normal curve is also plotted in this histogram, which allows you to see at a glance whether the distribution of scores is skewed to the left or to the right. In beginning any analysis, the first step is to run the frequencies of the responses for the different measures and develop a frequency table as well as a histogram to examine the variability and the normalcy of the curve.

Figure 6-7. Histogram

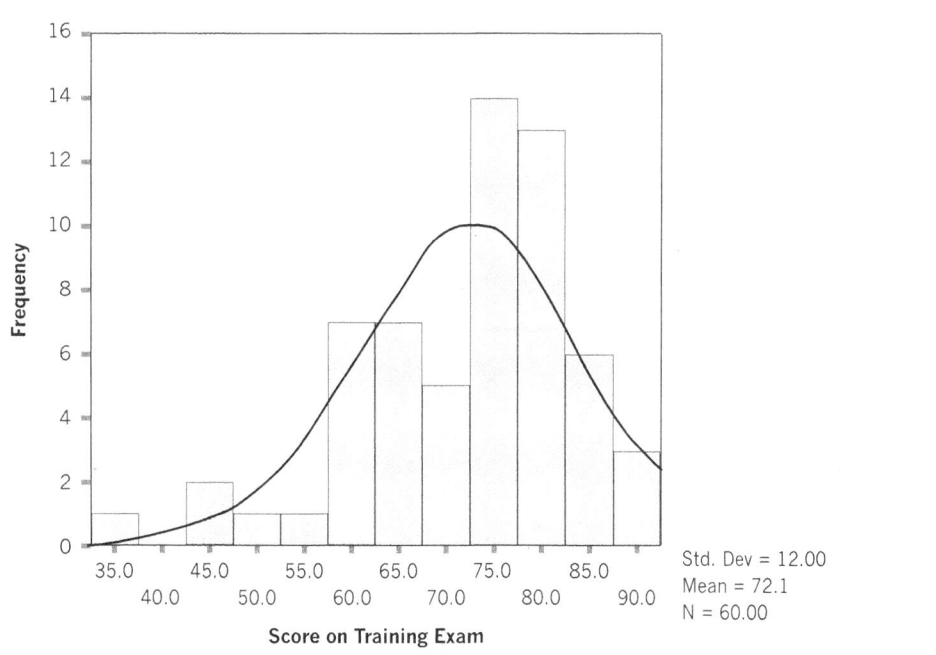

Box Plots

Box plots provide a display of data comparing groups of data and how the results compare on a variety of measures. In Figure 6-8 the box plot shows training exam scores for three groups. As you will notice for group number one, the test scores range from approximately 45 to 85. The box represents an interquartile containing 50 percent of the scores. The dark line in the middle of the box represents

155

Chapter 6

the median score that, in the case of group one, is 63.94. The standard deviation or the spread of scores is 13.5, which tells you there is a wide distribution of scores. Look at group two. The minimum score is not quite as low as in group one—47.56. The maximum score—89.65—is slightly higher than group one. The mean score is 73.57. The standard deviation for group two is 10.61, less variability. For group three, the minimum score—71.77—is well above the minimum scores for the other two groups. The maximum score—89.69—is just slightly above the maximum score for group two. The median score is 80.19. The standard deviation for group three is only 4.41, making both the box and the line between the minimum and maximum smaller than for either of the other two groups. Using box plots you can clearly communicate the difference among groups.

Figure 6-8. Box Plot

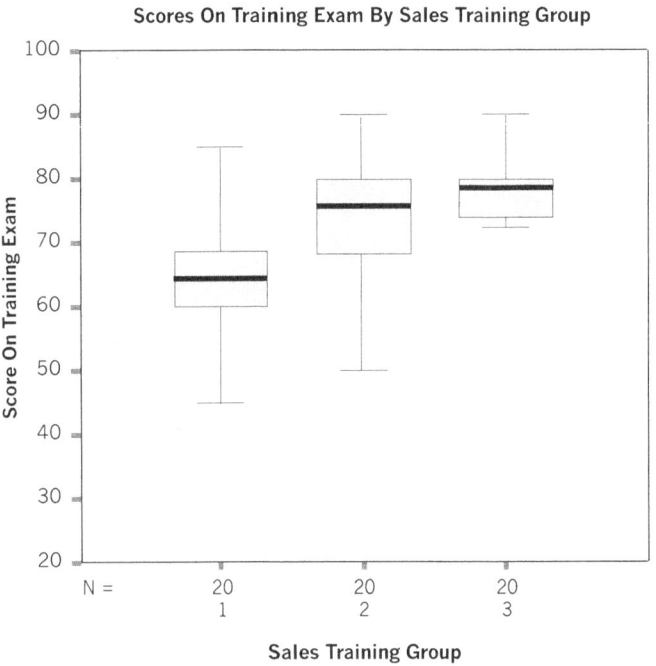

Line Graphs

A line graph is a good way to display multiple variables and how they compare. Figure 6-9 compares data provided by three different sources—participants of a training course, the supervisors of the participants, and the customers of the participants. The example displays the extent to which each source of data expects participants to apply the knowledge and skills gained during a training course. As shown, the supervisors have a higher expectation of performance for determining performance gaps, defining root causes, and reconciling requests than either the participant or the customer. The customer, on the other hand, has the lowest expectations for defining root causes, managing implementation, troubleshooting implementation, and recommending the right solution. Line graphs provide a simple depiction when comparing data from multiple sources on a variety of measures.

Figure 6-9. Line Graph

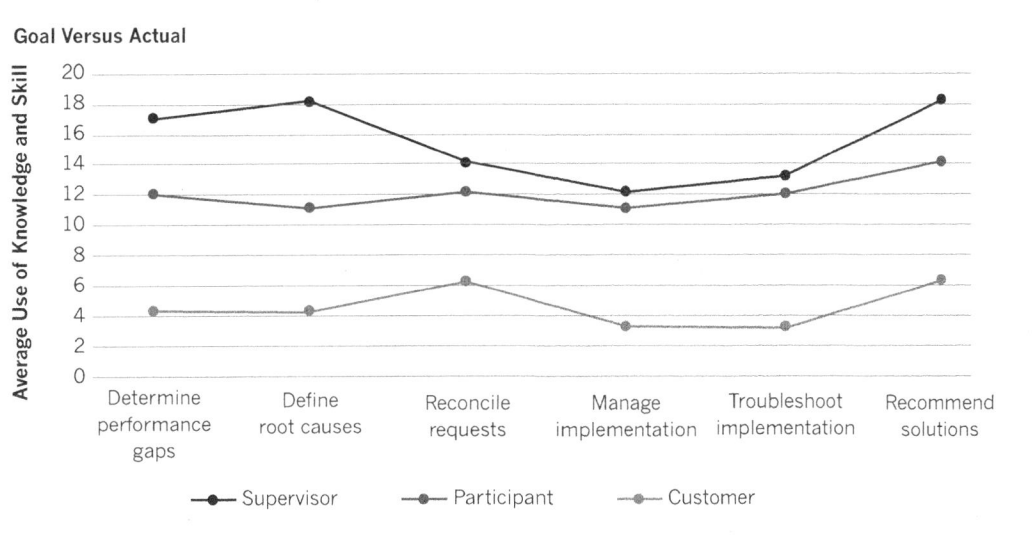

Graphical displays of data provide a concise reporting of results. They satisfy the need for those visual learners sitting at the executive table who may never hear a word you say, but who will respond to a picture!

Using Black Box Thinking to Improve Performance

The purpose of the ROI Methodology is not to simply report the return on investment of talent development programs. It is to identify and address opportunities to improve on successes or to correct disappointing outcomes, and avoid failures, using the outcome data from the process to take action.

Chapter 6

Consider how the airline industry processes information to respond to failures. Every aircraft is equipped with two almost-indestructible black boxes. One records instructions sent to the onboard electronic systems. The other records the conversations and sounds in the cockpit. If there is an accident, the boxes are opened, the data analyzed, and the reason for the accident pinpointed. This ensures procedures can be changed so that the same error never happens again. This is one of many reasons aircraft remains the safest mode of travel—industry leaders learn from failure.

Our thinking toward program evaluation should be as the airline industry's is to black box recordings. It's not enough to build in a process to record what goes on in an airplane cockpit—or before, during, and after a talent development program. Data lead to information that identifies problems and opportunities, which if addressed can drive performance improvement. Using black box thinking is thus an extension of telling your story because your story doesn't end with reporting results. It extends through using the Levels 1 through 5 data at the appropriate times.

Elevate the Conversation

Kent Barnett, founder of Perfomitiv, was correct when he said, "It's time to elevate the conversation with regard to learning analytics. Optimization of data is the next step in measurement." While the word *optimization* has been loosely thrown around for years, only a few companies really listen to and act on what the talent development measurement data tell them.

Take for example a faith-based nonprofit healthcare organization in Denver, Colorado, which is dedicated to improving the health of people and communities, especially those who are poor and vulnerable. Despite a –58 percent ROI on their clinical documentation program, they decided to continue the program because they believe that the long-term benefits and intangible benefits to the entire team will outweigh the costs. Additionally, and more importantly, upon looking at the data, they found that one group of participants outperformed the others by a significant amount. They decided to invest in creating a high-performer profile to help their talent acquisition team identify job candidates with the same characteristics. Now, they hire for the higher standard of performer and can raise the bar for their learning output. This is what we mean by optimization—learn from failure, use the data, and make improvement to the program, the organization that supports it, and the users of it.

Uses of Data

Sixty to 90 percent of job-related learning is wasted—that is, not used on the job, although participants may want to use it (Bran 2018). The primary culprit is system failure—that the system doesn't support or respect talent development. The system might not need the programs being offered, leaving talent development with a lack of control, no influence, and no seat at the table. While all of this, and more, may be true, playing the victim doesn't cut it. The purpose of talent development and measurement, evaluation, and analytics is to nudge people toward action that will lead to improvement in organization performance. No more, no less.

Good measurement and evaluation addresses the right questions, the right way, and provides insights into the actions we can take to do our job well. Table 6-7 summarizes a few uses of evaluation data at the five levels.

Table 6-7. Uses of Evaluation Data

Use of Evaluation Data	Appropriate Level of Data				
	1	2	3	4	5
Adjust program design	✓	✓			
Improve program delivery	✓	✓			
Influence application and impact				✓	✓
Enhance reinforcement			✓		
Improve management support			✓	✓	
Improve stakeholder satisfaction			✓	✓	✓
Recognize and reward participants		✓	✓	✓	
Justify or enhance budget				✓	✓
Develop norms and standards	✓	✓	✓		
Reduce costs		✓	✓	✓	✓
Market programs	✓		✓	✓	✓
Expand implementation to other areas				✓	✓

When to Act

Changes are made at different points based on data collected during the talent development process. In the initial stages it is important to have the right people involved in a program at the right time. Among other things, this means that an opportunity must exist in their work for them to use what they learn through a program or project. This type of information is collected and validated with Level 0: Input data.

Level 1: Reaction and Planned Action data and Level 2: Learning data determine whether the program content matters to participants. Once a program is underway, assessment of buy-in begins. At any point in time, if there is reason to believe that participants do not see value in a program, adjustments must be made. The same is true with knowledge acquisition. If evidence exists that participants "get it" and the intent is for them to "use it," it is time to act. Participants must be willing and able to do what they need to do as a result of the program; otherwise, there will be no impact and no ROI.

Application and implementation of knowledge acquired must take place—the program must be designed to stick. Success is determined through Level 3 measurement. Unfortunately, it is at this stage where the chain of value most frequently breaks. Participants don't use what they learn for a variety reasons, many of which are out of the direct control of talent development, but all of which can be influenced by talent development. When these barriers come to light, action must be taken to change the system that should be supporting learning transfer.

In addition to barriers of application, there are enabling factors. Identification of these factors through Level 3 measurement offers another opportunity to act. Replication of what works is just as important as addressing what does not work.

Another point at which action should be taken is when the Level 4: Impact results become evident. For some program evaluations, these measures improve, and it is important to know why. If the program caused the improvement, this is good news, and the action to follow is to share that news and devise a plan to replicate or enhance success. But if the program did not cause it and the improvement is due to other factors, the question is why not. Taking action to understand the underlying reason for program failure is the epitome of black box thinking.

A final point at which action should be taken is based on Level 5: ROI. Sometimes the ROI will be quite high. That is not the time to sit on your laurels. Extremely high ROIs mean there is something going on that is making the program work. It might be because the problem the program addressed was so bad and so expensive that any simple solution would make a difference. But it could also be because the program was rolled out in such a way that the system supported it. The questions to be answered here are why and how. Replicating this success in other areas will prove beneficial.

On the other hand, a program may also lead to a negative ROI. This is time to act—and quite frankly, this is a point at which the most action tends to occur. When a negative ROI occurs, it is not the time to duck under that rock; it is the time to find out what happened and take action to prevent it from happening again.

Optimization is an act, process, or methodology of making something as fully perfect, functional, or effective as possible. That is what talent development is all about; and to do its job, talent development needs measurement, evaluation, and ROI.

Getting It Done

This chapter concludes the steps in the ROI Methodology: from planning the evaluation, to collecting data, analyzing them, and optimizing results. Now you have three actions you need to take. First, continue filling out your ROI analysis plan, which you started in chapter 4 and worked on in chapter 5. Complete the last two columns—"Communication Targets" and "Other Influences" (things that may affect the outcomes of the program or may affect the evaluation). Second, develop a communication plan, answering the following questions:

- **What do you need from your communication?** In answering this question, go back to the purpose of your evaluation. What are you trying to do? Improve the program? Ask for additional funding? Discontinue a program? Remember, there could be multiple needs.
- **Whom do you ask?** Who is the best audience for this communication? Remember that there are four key audiences to whom you will always communicate results. Is there another group with whom you need to communicate in order to address your need?
- **How do you plan to ask?** Are you going to set up a meeting or post something on the organization's intranet?

Your communication plan will have a variety of the reasons for the communication, the audience you plan to address, and communication delivery methodologies.

In order to move forward with the content of this chapter, complete the communication plan in Exercise 6-1. This will ensure that you develop the right reports for the right purposes, targeting the right audiences, and using the most appropriate methods of distribution.

Your third action is to reflect on how well you and your team employ black box thinking. Do you? If you do, how well is it working? If not, why not?

Chapter 7 wraps up *ROI Basics* by offering ideas for how you can seamlessly integrate the ROI Methodology into your talent development practices.

Exercise 6-1. Sample Communication Plan

Need for Communication	Target Audience	Communication Document	Distribution Method

7

Sustain Momentum

What's Inside This Chapter

Now that you know the basics of developing an ROI impact study, it's time to learn how to keep up the momentum. This includes:
- identifying resistance to implementation
- overcoming resistance to implementation
- making the ROI Methodology routine.

7

Sustain Momentum

Identifying Resistance

Resistance to comprehensive evaluation like the ROI Methodology will be based on fear, lack of understanding, opposition to change, and the efforts required to make a change successful. To not only identify resistance but overcome it, you need to start with the talent development team, go to the management team, and then do a gap analysis.

Start With the Talent Development Team

The biggest resistance will probably come from within the talent development team. As Pogo, the famous comic strip character, once said, "We have met the enemy, and he is us." The staff may resist the extra efforts required to use ROI on the talent development process. The problems, concerns, or fears that arise must be uncovered.

Feedback from the talent development staff should be collected from formal meetings or questionnaires aimed at uncovering the areas of concern. What are the pressure points? What are the issues? What are the problems? They will quickly surface in this type of meeting or instrument. It is best to get all problems, concerns, and fears out in the open so that they can be addressed.

Also collect informal feedback from the individuals whose support is needed for the ROI process to work properly. Pay particular attention to those recognized as official or unofficial leaders. Formal assessment, feedback on concerns, and informal feedback expose many of the staff's issues with ROI. Table 7-1 shows typical statements of resistance.

Some of these concerns are realistic; others are not. Implementing the ROI Methodology will, no doubt, take additional effort and generate change in the way in which talent development is implemented in the organization. This process will require making painful changes when programs are not living up to expectations. However, this process also has many positive outcomes. Yet, because of the concerns or fears, individuals may not be able to see the positive.

For most implementations, many of the concerns about ROI are based on either lack of understanding or belief in the myths about ROI—a problem that can easily be confronted in a proper implementation process.

Table 7-1. Typical Objections to ROI.

• This costs too much.	• I do not understand this.	• The ROI process is too subjective.
• We don't need this.	• Our clients will never buy this.	• Our managers will not support this.
• This takes too much time.	• What happens when the results are negative?	• ROI is too narrowly focused.
• Who is asking for this?	• How can we be consistent with this?	• This is not practical.
• This is not in my job duties.		
• I did not have input on this.		

Go to the Management Team

The management team presents its own resistance challenges and will have questions about talent development that must be analyzed and addressed. The first issue to recognize is that different levels of management have different concerns about the talent development process and ROI. Are the immediate managers of participants involved? If so, then their concerns should be addressed. Sometimes, the middle level of management, those who budget for talent development and support it in a variety of ways, may be the target. At other times, the concerns may come from top management where the ultimate commitment to talent development is crystallized. These individuals decide to what extent the talent development function exists by providing the necessary resources and by supporting the process with highly visible actions.

Once the target is identified, the next step is to collect feedback. Meetings and questionnaires are also appropriate for the management team. The responses can reveal much about management's perceptions of the success of the talent development process. The results quickly show concerns and areas where action is needed.

Others who are involved may have concerns that you should address. If there are outsourcing partners, input should be obtained from them as well. External groups, such as customer groups, involved with talent development should also be included. The important issue is to make sure that those involved in supporting and sustaining the talent development process will have opportunities to sort out their concerns. Table 7-2 shows these groups' typical reactions to accountability issues and efforts, which may be surprising to the talent development staff.

Table 7-2. Typical Accountability Reactions

Accountability Issues	Reaction to ROI
• Is all this training really needed?	• Is this more new jargon?
• How is talent development helping our business?	• Is this the ROI that I know?
• Can we do this with less cost?	• How can you do this?
• Do we have what it takes?	• Why didn't you do this earlier?
• Why does this take so long?	• Is this credible?
• Show me the money.	• Can we do this for every program?

Conduct a Gap Analysis

Given the concerns from the staff and various support and stakeholder groups, you should conduct a gap analysis. A gap analysis focuses on where things are compared to where they need to be—for example, where management support is versus where it needs to be for the ROI process to work. It may be helpful to conduct gap analyses in a variety of different areas as shown in Table 7-3.

Table 7-3. Typical Gap Categories

• Staff capability for ROI	• Appropriate environment for transfer of learning
• Results-based talent development	• Effective management support
• Alignment with business needs	• The perception of value of talent development
• Effective policies, procedures, and templates	

One of the most important issues is to assess the staff's capability with ROI. If there is a gap between actual versus needed knowledge and understanding of ROI, specific actions must be taken so that all individuals involved will be on track to use the process properly.

Another area that may need adjustment is the talent development cycle. Evaluation must be considered early and often in the cycle. Data collection may need to be built into some processes, requiring participants and others to provide data as part of the learning process.

A third area of concern is business alignment—the extent to which programs are presently aligned to the business when compared to the best possible alignment. Often you must change practices and processes so that programs are more directly linked to business needs from the very beginning.

Policies, procedures, and guidelines often have to be changed so that evaluation becomes standardized, consistent, and routine. Policies and guidelines include statements about the percentage of programs that will be taken to various levels of evaluation, the extent of up-front business alignment with programs, and other important procedures.

Another important area to assess is the gap between reality and expectation in the workplace, which has to be analyzed and often changed to support the transfer of learning. In the initial analysis, the workplace must be free of barriers to learning transfer. Supporters and enablers should be in place to assist the transfer of learning from a program to on-the-job application. You should consider learning transfer issues before, during, and after programs are designed and implemented.

Next, management support is a key issue and specific efforts may be needed to improve support on different levels. To get managers involved, make sure they have the appropriate information and show them what the talent development process is doing for them. A variety of support processes can make a difference in the success or failure of a program.

Finally, perceptions have to change—perceptions about the value of the talent development process and its contribution to the organization. Although the change may take time and require clear and wide-ranging evidence of success, it is necessary. With this gap analysis, the specific steps can be taken to narrow and close these gaps, so that you can overcome resistance to accountability efforts.

Overcoming Resistance to Implementation

To overcome resistance requires a methodical approach with a variety of actions to remove, minimize, or go around the barriers and problems identified in the gap analysis. When you overcome the resistance, you can accomplish implementation. Figure 7-1 shows the building blocks necessary to overcome the resistance to ROI implementation. The building blocks are approached from the first actions at the bottom of the figure to the last actions on the top, so that each block can be put in place before moving to the next.

Figure 7-1. Building Blocks for Overcoming Resistance

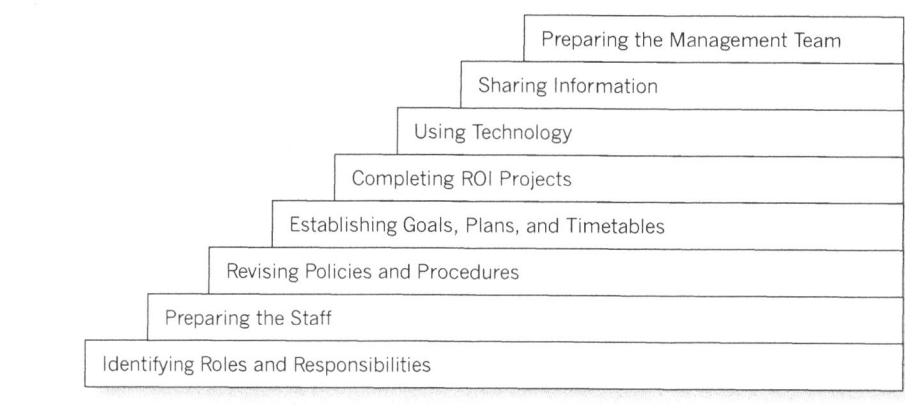

Identifying Roles and Responsibilities

A variety of roles and responsibilities are required to achieve successful implementation. An important role is the ROI champion who helps identify and delegate important responsibilities to ensure successful implementation.

Identifying a Champion

As a first step in the process, one or more individuals should be designated as the internal leader for ROI. As in most change efforts, someone must take responsibility for ensuring that the process is implemented successfully. The ROI champion is usually the one who understands the process best and sees the potential of the ROI Methodology. This leader must be willing to teach and coach others. Table 7-4 presents the various roles of the ROI champion.

Table 7-4. Roles of the ROI Champion

• Technical expert	• Consultant	• Developer	• Teacher	• Process monitor
• Initiator	• Designer	• Cheerleader	• Communicator	• Interpreter
• Coordinator	• Problem solver	• Planner	• Analyst	

The ROI leader is usually a member of the talent development staff who has this responsibility full time in larger organizations or part time in smaller organizations. The typical job title for a full-time ROI leader is manager or leader of measurement and evaluation. Some organizations assign this responsibility to a team and empower them to lead the ROI effort.

Delegating Responsibilities to Ensure Success

Determining specific responsibilities is a critical issue because there can be confusion when individuals are unclear about their specific assignments in the ROI process. Responsibilities fall into two broad groups. The first group is the measurement and evaluation responsibility for the entire talent development staff. This group is involved in designing, developing, delivering, coordinating, and supporting programs; providing input on the design of instruments; planning an evaluation; collecting data; and interpreting the results. Typical responsibilities include:

- ensuring that the needs assessment includes specific business results measures
- developing specific Level 3: Application objectives and Level 4: Impact objectives for each program
- focusing the content of the program on performance improvement—ensuring that exercises, tests, case studies, and skill practices relate to the desired objectives
- keeping participants focused on application and results objectives
- communicating rationale and reasons for evaluation
- assisting in follow-up activities to capture application and impact results data
- providing assistance for data collection, data analysis, and reporting
- developing plans for data collection and analysis
- presenting evaluation data to a variety of groups
- helping with the design of instruments.

Although it may be inappropriate to have each member of the staff involved in all of these activities, each individual should have at least one or more responsibilities as part of routine job duties. This assignment of responsibility keeps the ROI process from being disjointed and separate from major talent development activities. More important, it brings accountability to those who develop, deliver, and implement the programs.

The second group is the technical support function. Depending on the size of the talent development staff, it may be helpful to have technical experts provide assistance with the ROI Methodology. These experts supplement technical expertise, not relieve others of evaluation responsibilities. Some organizations have found this approach to be effective. When this type of support is developed, responsibilities revolve around eight key areas:

- designing data collection instruments
- providing assistance for developing an evaluation strategy
- coordinating a major evaluation project
- analyzing data, including specialized statistical analyses

Chapter 7

- interpreting results and making specific recommendations
- developing an evaluation report or case study to communicate overall results
- presenting results to critical audiences
- providing technical support in any phase of the ROI process.

Who is responsible for each part of the evaluation needs attention throughout the process. It is not unusual to require others in support functions to be responsible for data collection. These responsibilities are defined when a particular evaluation strategy plan is developed and approved.

 Noted

It will only take 3 to 5 percent of your talent development budget to create and integrate a robust measurement and evaluation practice. That's pennies compared to value of the opportunities lost if you don't have one.

Preparing the Staff

Staff preparation is critical. Working with evaluation is a new endeavor for many leaders as well as talent development staff. For this reason, it is important to consider what knowledge, skills, and experiences the leaders and staff need to ensure successful implementation.

Developing the ROI Leaders

In preparation for the assignment to ROI leaders, individuals usually obtain special training to build specific skills and knowledge in the ROI Methodology. The role of the implementation leader serves a variety of specialized duties.

At times, the ROI implementation leader serves as technical expert, giving advice and making decisions about some of the issues involved in evaluation design, data analysis, and presentation. As an initiator, the leader identifies programs for ROI analysis and takes the lead in conducting a variety of ROI studies. When needed, the implementation leader is a cheerleader, bringing attention to the ROI process, encouraging others to become involved, and showing how value can be added to the organization. The implementation leader is also a communicator—letting others know about the process and communicating results to target audiences. All the roles can come into play at one time or another as the leader implements ROI in the organization.

Developing the Staff

A group that will often resist the ROI Methodology is the staff who must design, develop, deliver, and coordinate talent development solutions. These staff members often see evaluation as an unnecessary intrusion into their responsibilities—absorbing precious time and stifling their freedom to be creative.

You should involve the staff on each key issue in the process. As policy statements are prepared and evaluation guidelines developed, staff input is essential. It is difficult for the staff to be critical of something they helped design, develop, and plan. Using meetings, brainstorming sessions, and task forces, the staff should be involved in every phase of developing the framework and supporting documents for ROI. In an ideal situation, the staff can learn the process in a two-day workshop and, at the same time, develop guidelines, policy, and application targets. This approach is very efficient, completing several tasks at the same time.

Using ROI As a Learning Tool—Not a Performance Evaluation Tool

One reason the staff may resist the ROI Methodology is that the effectiveness of their programs will be fully exposed, placing their reputation on the line. They may have a fear of failure. To overcome this, the process should clearly be positioned as a tool for process improvement and not a tool to evaluate talent development staff performance, at least during its early years of implementation. Talent development staff will not be interested in developing a tool that will be used to expose their shortcomings and failures.

Evaluators can learn more from failures than from successes. If the program is not working, it is best to find this out quickly and understand the issues. If a program is ineffective, it will eventually be known to the clients and the management group, if they are not aware of it already. Lack of results will cause managers to become less supportive of talent development. Dwindling support appears in many forms, ranging from reducing budgets to refusing to let participants be involved in programs. If the weaknesses of programs are identified and adjustments are made quickly, not only will effective programs be developed, but also the credibility and respect for the function and the staff will be enhanced.

Revising Policies and Procedures

Another key part of implementation is revising the organization's policy concerning measurement and evaluation, often a part of policy and practice for developing and implementing talent development programs. The policy statement contains information developed specifically for the measurement and evaluation process. It is frequently developed with the input of the talent development staff, key managers or sponsors, and the finance and accounting staff. Sometimes policy issues are addressed during internal workshops designed to build skills with measurement and evaluation. Table 7-5 shows the topics in the measurement and evaluation policy for a large organization.

Table 7-5. Results-Based Internal Talent Development Policy

1. Purpose.
2. Mission.
3. Evaluate all programs, which will include the following levels:
   - Level 1: Reaction and Planned Action (100%)
   - Level 2: Learning (no less than 70%)
   - Level 3: Application and Implementation (50%)
   - Level 4: Impact (usually through sampling) (10%) (highly visible, expensive)
   - Level 5: ROI (7%).
4. Evaluation support group (corporate) will provide assistance and advice in measurement and evaluation, instrument design, data analysis, and evaluation strategy.
5. New programs are developed following logical steps beginning with needs analysis and ending with communicating results.
6. Evaluation instruments must be designed or selected to collect data for evaluation. They must be valid, reliable, economical, and subject to audit by evaluation support group.
7. Responsibility for talent development program results rests with facilitators, participants, and supervisors of participants.
8. An adequate system for collecting and monitoring talent development costs must be in place. All direct costs should be included.
9. At least annually, the management board will review the status and results of talent development. The review will include plans, strategies, results, costs, priorities, and concerns.
10. Line management shares in the responsibility for program evaluation through follow-up, pre-program commitments, and overall support.
11. Managers and supervisors must declare competence achieved through talent development programs. When not applicable, the talent development staff should evaluate.
12. External consultants must be selected based on previous evaluation data. A central data or resource base should exist.
13. All external programs of more than one day in duration will be subjected to evaluation procedures. In addition, participants will assess the quality of external programs.
14. Talent development program results must be communicated to the appropriate target audience. As a minimum, this includes management (participants' supervisors), participants, and all learning staff.
15. Key talent development staff members should be qualified to do effective needs analysis and evaluation.
16. A central database for program development must be in place to prevent duplication and serve as program resource.
17. Union involvement is necessary in total talent development plan.

The policy statement addresses critical issues that will influence the effectiveness of the measurement and evaluation process. Typical topics include adopting the five-level evaluation framework presented in this book; requiring objectives at the higher levels at least for some, if not all, programs; and defining responsibilities for talent development.

Policy statements guide and direct the staff and others who work closely with the ROI Methodology. They keep the process clearly focused and enable the group to establish goals for evaluation. They also provide an opportunity to communicate basic requirements and fundamental issues regarding performance and accountability. More than anything else, policy statements serve as a learning tool to teach others, especially when they are developed in a collaborative and collective way. If policy statements are developed in isolation and do not have the ownership of the staff and management, they will not be effective or useful.

Guidelines and processes for measurement and evaluation are important to show how to use the tools and techniques, guide the design process, provide consistency in the ROI Methodology, ensure that appropriate methods are used, and place the proper emphasis on each of the areas. The guidelines are more technical than policy statements and often contain detailed procedures showing how the process is undertaken and developed. They often include specific forms, instruments, and tools necessary to facilitate the process.

Establishing Goals, Plans, and Timetables

As pointed out in chapter 2, planning is a critical part of the process—plan your work; work your plan. This rings true with taking steps to sustain your evaluation practice, such as setting targets and developing a project plan.

Setting Targets

Establishing specific targets for evaluation levels is an important way to make progress with measurement and evaluation. Targets enable the staff to focus on the improvements needed with specific evaluation levels. In this process, the percentage of programs planned for evaluation at each level is developed. The first step is to assess the present situation. The number of all programs, including repeated sections of a program, is tabulated along with the corresponding level of evaluation presently conducted for each course. Next, the percentage of courses using Level 1: Reaction questionnaires is calculated. The process is repeated for each level of the evaluation. The current percentages for Levels 3, 4, and 5 are usually low.

After detailing the current situation, the next step is to determine a realistic target for each level within a specific timeframe. Many organizations set annual targets for changes. This process should involve the input of the talent development staff to ensure that the targets are realistic and that the staff is committed to the process and targets. If the talent development staff does not develop ownership for this process, targets will not be met. The improvement targets must be achievable, while at the same time, challenging and motivating. Table 7-6 shows the recommended annual targets for evaluation at the five levels.

Table 7-6. Evaluation Targets

Level of Evaluation	Percentage of Programs Evaluated at This Level
Level 1: Reaction and Planned Action	90–100%
Level 2: Learning	60–90%
Level 3: Application and Implementation	30–40%
Level 4: Impact	10–20%
Level 5: ROI	5–10%

Using this example, 90 to 100 percent of the programs are measured at Level 1, which is consistent with many other organizations. Only 60 to 90 percent of the programs are measured at Level 2 using a formal method of measurement. At this level, informal methods are not counted as a learning measure. Level 3 represents a 30 to 40 percent follow-up. Ten to 20 percent are planned for evaluation at Level 4 and half of those are planned for evaluation to Level 5. These percentages are typical and often recommended.

Target setting is a critical implementation issue. It should be completed early in the process with full support of the talent development staff. Also, if practical and feasible, the targets should have the approval of the key management staff, particularly the senior management team.

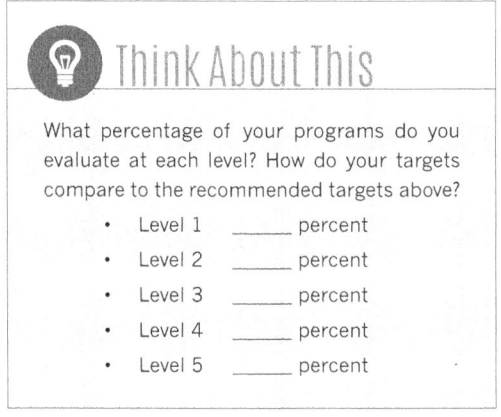

Developing a Project Plan

An important part of the planning process is to establish timetables for the complete implementation process. The timetables become a master plan for completing the different elements, beginning with assigning responsibilities and concluding with meeting the targets previously described. Figure 7-2 shows an ROI implementation project plan for a large petroleum company.

From a practical basis, this schedule is a project plan for transition from the present situation to a desired future situation. The more detailed the document, the more useful it will become.

The project plan is a living, long-range document that should be reviewed frequently and adjusted as necessary. More important, it should always be familiar to those who are routinely working with the ROI Methodology.

Figure 7-2. ROI Implementation Project Plan for a Large Petroleum Company

	J	F	M	A	M	J	J	A	S	O	N	D	J	F	M	A	M	J	J	A	S	O	N
Team Formed	■																						
Policy Developed		■	■																				
Targets Set	■																						
Network Formed			■																				
Workshops Developed				■	■	■																	
ROI Project (A)					■	■	■	■															
ROI Project (B)						■	■	■	■														
ROI Project (C)								■	■	■	■												
ROI Project (D)									■	■	■	■											
WLP Staff Trained							■	■	■														
Suppliers Trained											■	■	■										
Managers Trained																	■	■	■				
Support Tools Developed					■	■																	
Evaluation Guidelines Developed				■	■																		

Completing ROI Projects

The next major step is to complete the ROI projects. A small number of projects are usually initiated, perhaps two or three programs. The selected programs most often represent the functional areas of the business, such as operations, sales, finance, engineering, and information systems. It is important to select a manageable number so the projects will be completed.

Ultimately, the number of programs tackled depends on the resources available to conduct the studies, as well as the internal need for accountability. Using the profile above, for an organization with 200 programs, this means that 10 to 20 percent (20 to 40) of the programs will have Level 4: Impact and/or Level 5: ROI results studies conducted annually.

As the projects are developed and the ROI implementation is under way, status meetings should be conducted to report progress and discuss critical issues with appropriate team members. For example, if a leadership program is selected as one of the ROI projects, all the key staff involved in the program (design, development, and delivery) should meet regularly to discuss the status of the project. This keeps the project team focused on the critical issues, generates the best ideas to tackle problems and barriers, and builds a knowledge base to implement evaluation in future programs.

 **Noted**

Not every offering of a program is evaluated to impact or ROI. This type of evaluation is typically conducted on select offerings. So, while 20 unique programs may be targeted for ROI evaluation, it is likely only one or two will be evaluated to those levels.

These meetings serve three major purposes: reporting progress, learning, and planning. The meeting usually begins with a status report on each ROI project, describing what has been accomplished since the previous meeting. Next, discussions take place about the specific barriers and problems encountered. During the discussions, new tactics, techniques, or tools are brought up. Also, the entire group discusses how to remove barriers to success and focuses on suggestions and recommendations for next steps, including developing specific plans. Finally, the next steps are developed, discussed, and configured. Ultimately, these projects must be completed, and the results communicated to the appropriate audiences.

Using Technology

To ensure the measurement and evaluation are efficiently and effectively administered will require the use of technology. Throughout this book, a few types of technologies that support evaluation were mentioned. Technologies can range from simple, inexpensive software purchases to complete systems for managing large amounts of data. Five areas are often addressed when technology is considered in the context of measurement and evaluation.

First, the data collected for Level 1 and the self-assessments at Level 2 need to be managed efficiently using technology. Because of the high percentage of programs evaluated, technology must be used so that data administration and integration will not consume too many resources. A variety of tools are available ranging from using scannable documents to subscription software for processing Levels 1 and 2 data on an outsource basis. This level of data requires only simple analysis.

The second area involves Level 2 data that goes beyond the self-assessment applications. Designing tests that are more objective and checking the validity and reliability of tests may require test design software, ranging from simple test construction software to detailed software for designing all types of tests, including simulations.

The third area is software for follow-up evaluations. This often involves the use of surveys, interviews, and focus group information. A variety of software packages are available to process data from surveys and questionnaires, including qualitative analysis for focus groups and interviews.

The fourth area of consideration is software for conducting detailed results studies. Some software packages are available to carry out experimental research designs, such as a control group analysis, while others are designed to automate ROI studies using questionnaires and action plans.

Fifth, your organization's learning management system may provide some, if not all, of the technology needed to administer the management and evaluation processes. Many learning management system providers have built-in evaluation tools or links to the most common available tools to manage the data needed for Levels 1, 2, and 3, and sometimes even 4 and 5, in the analysis.

In short, technology is an important way to ease implementation. Appropriate use of technology reduces the amount of time to collect, tabulate, analyze, and report data. When time is minimized, implementation is much easier.

Sharing Information

Because the ROI Methodology is new to many individuals, it is helpful to have a peer group experiencing similar issues and frustrations. Tapping into an international network, joining or creating a local network, or building an internal network are all possible ways to use the resources, ideas, and support of others.

One way to integrate the information needs of talent development professionals for an effective ROI evaluation process is through an internal ROI network. The concept of a network is simplicity itself. The idea is to bring people who are interested in ROI together throughout the organization to work under the guidance of trained ROI evaluators. Typically, advocates within the department see both the need for beginning networks and the potential of ROI evaluation to change how the department does its work. Interested network members learn by designing and executing real evaluation plans. This process generates commitment for accountability as a new way of doing business for the department.

Chapter 7

Preparing the Management Team

Several actions can be taken with the management team to ensure that they are supporting evaluation and using the data properly. In some cases, they need to understand more about ROI. Four specific efforts need to be considered.

First, present data to the management team routinely so that they understand the value of talent development, particularly Level 3: Application and Implementation, which translates directly into new skills in the workplace, and Level 4: Impact, which relates directly to goals and key performance indicators. The management team also needs Level 5: ROI, which shows the value of learning compared to the cost. Having routine information in these areas helps them build an appreciation for the value of talent development so that their support will increase in the future.

Second, get your management team more involved in the evaluation process. In addition to reviewing data, managers may be asked to help make decisions about the fate of, or adjustments to, a program. They may be needed in collecting some of the data and supporting data collection efforts. In some cases, they may be specifying what data are needed, including assisting with the up-front business alignment. Manager input is needed throughout the accountability cycle, from the initial business alignment to setting objectives to assisting with evaluation.

Third, ensure managers get full credit for improvements. Although this is a communication and reporting issue, it is critical that managers support accountability efforts in the future. All the improvements in the workplace (which generated the ROI) should be credited to the proper individuals, with the key manager being the person responsible for it. If the talent development function takes credit for the success of the program, the relationship can sour quickly. Give the praise where it is deserved and needed.

Fourth, teach or brief managers on the ROI Methodology. Managers need to understand what the process is about and what it can do—and not do—for them. They need to understand the resources involved in conducting credible ROI studies, so they can help the talent development staff use this tool more selectively. To accomplish this, the organization might offer a special workshop, "Manager's Role in Talent Development." Varying in duration from half day to two days, this workshop can shape critical skills and change perceptions to enhance the support of the ROI Methodology. After, managers will have an improved perception of the impact of learning, a more clear understanding of their role in the talent development process, and often a renewed commitment to make learning work in their organization.

Making the ROI Methodology Routine

After the ROI Methodology is implemented in the organization, it must be sustained; it must become routine so that it doesn't deteriorate and fade away. Making it routine requires building it into a process perceived as necessary, essential, and almost effortless. This section reviews the key steps designed to make it routine.

For lasting value, measurement, evaluation, and ROI must not be seen as a one-time event or an add-on process. Evaluation studies must be planned and integrated into the talent development process as early as possible. The tasks, processes, and procedures of evaluation must be painless, which will increase the odds that they will be used regularly. When evaluation becomes routine, it will become an accepted and important—and sometimes required—element in the talent development cycle.

Making Planning Routine

Intuitively, most professionals realize that planning is an important way to minimize problems, reduce resources, and stay focused on the outcome. Nowhere is this more true than when planning a comprehensive evaluation. Planning minimizes the time required later, keeps the evaluation efficient and less expensive, and helps all stakeholders to become focused on tasks and processes. It also serves to gain buy-in from key clients and makes evaluation routine.

Planning is essential whenever a major evaluation study is conducted. Even if the program has been operational for some time and the evaluation is suddenly requested, planning is needed to decide how to collect, process, and report data. Ideally, the evaluation plan should be in place before the talent development program is operational so that the planning may influence its design, development, and delivery.

Implementing and communicating the evaluation plan is the next step to making planning routine. This means detailing the sequence of events as they should occur from the time that the evaluation plan is developed until all the evaluation results have been communicated.

These planning documents can be completed in a matter of hours when the various team members and stakeholders are available to provide input. The payoff is tremendous, as planning not only makes the process faster and more efficient, but also enhances the likelihood that it will become routine.

Integrating Evaluation Into Talent Development Programs

One of the most effective ways to make evaluation routine is to build it into the program. This approach changes the perception of evaluation from an add-on process to one that is an integral part of the application of learning. It means going beyond reaction and learning evaluation data, the capture of which is usually built into the talent development programs.

Built-in evaluations can be accomplished in several ways. One of the most effective is to use action plans that serve as application tools for the knowledge and skills learned in the program. The action plan is included as part of the program, and its requirement is communicated early. Appropriate agenda time is taken to explain how to develop and use the action plan and, ideally, participants are provided program time to complete it. The follow-up on the success of the action plan provides data for evaluation. In this context, the action plan becomes an application tool instead of an evaluation tool. The commitment to the participants is that the completed action plan data will be summarized for the entire sample group and returned to them so that each member can see what others have accomplished. This provides a little of "what's in it for me" for the participants. Action plans are used to drive not only application and implementation data, but also impact data.

Another built-in technique is to integrate the follow-up questionnaire with the talent development program. Ample time should be provided to review the items on the questionnaire and secure a commitment to provide data. This step-by-step review of expectations helps clarify confusing issues and improves response rates as participants make a commitment to provide the data. This easy-to-accomplish step can be a powerful way to enhance data collection. It prevents the need for constant reminders to participants to provide data at a later follow-up date.

Using Shortcuts

One of the most significant barriers to the implementation of measurement and evaluation is the potential time and cost involved in implementing the process. An important tradeoff exists between the task of additional analysis versus the use of shortcut methods, including estimation. In those tradeoffs, shortcuts win almost every time. An increasing amount of research shows shortcuts and estimates, when provided by those who know a process best (experts), can be even more accurate than more sophisticated, detailed analysis. Essentially, evaluators try to avoid the high costs of increasing accuracy because it just doesn't pay off.

Sometimes, the perception of excessive time and cost is only a myth; at other times, it is a reality. Most organizations can implement the evaluation methodology for about 3 percent to 5 percent of the talent development budget. Nevertheless, evaluation still commands significant time and monetary resources. A variety of approaches have commanded much attention recently and represent an important part of the implementation strategy.

Take Shortcuts at Lower Levels

When resources are a primary concern and shortcuts need to be taken, it is best to take them at lower levels in the evaluation scheme. This is a resource allocation issue. For example, if Level 4: Impact evaluation is conducted, Levels 1 to 3 do not have to be as comprehensive. This shift places most of the emphasis on the highest level of the evaluation.

Fund Measurement and Evaluation With Program Cost Savings

Almost every ROI impact study generates data from which to make improvements. Results at different levels often show how the program can be altered or completely redesigned to make it more effective and efficient. These actions can lead to cost savings. In a few cases, the program may have to be eliminated because it is not adding value and no amount of adjustment will result in program improvement. In this case, substantial cost savings can be realized as the program is eliminated. A logical argument can be made to shift a portion of these savings to fund additional measurement and evaluation. Some organizations gradually migrate to a budget target of 5 percent for measurement and evaluation spending by using the savings generated from the use of evaluation. This provides a disciplined and conservative approach to additional funding.

As a percentage of the total talent development budget, how much do you currently spend on evaluation? What will it take to increase your funding?

Use Participants

One of the most effective cost-saving approaches is to have participants conduct major steps of the process. Participants are the primary source for understanding the degree to which learning is applied and has driven success on the job. The responsibilities for the participants should be expanded from the traditional requirement of involvement in learning activities and application of new skills. They must be asked to show the impact of those new skills and provide data about success as a routine part of the process. Consequently, the role of the participant can be expanded from learning and application to measuring the impact and communicating information.

Use Sampling

Not all programs require comprehensive evaluation, nor should all participants necessarily be evaluated in a planned follow-up. Thus, sampling can be used in two ways. First, you may select only a few programs for Levels 4 and 5 evaluation. Those programs should be selected based on the criteria described earlier in this book. Next, when a program is evaluated, in most cases, only a sample of participants should be evaluated to keep costs and time to a minimum.

Use Estimates

Estimates are an important part of the process. They are also the least expensive way to arrive at a number or value. Whether isolating the effects of the talent development program or converting data to monetary value, estimates can be a routine and credible part of the process. The important point is to make sure the estimate is credible and follows systematic, logical, and consistent steps.

Use Internal Resources

An organization does not necessarily have to employ consultants to develop ROI studies and address other measurement and evaluation issues. Internal capability can be developed, eliminating the need to depend on consultants, which can reduce costs. This approach is perhaps one of the most significant timesavers. The difference in using internal resources versus external consultants can save as much as 50 to 60 percent of the costs of a specific project.

Use Standard Templates

Most organizations don't have the time or resources to customize each evaluation project. To the extent possible, develop standard instruments that can be used over and over. If customization is needed, it is only a minor part of it. For example, the reaction questionnaire should be standardized and automated to save time and to make evaluation routine. Learning measurements can be standard and built into the reaction evaluation questionnaire, unless methods that are more objective are needed, such as testing, simulation, and skill practices. Follow-up evaluation questionnaires can be standard, with only a part of the questionnaire being customized. Patterned interviews can be developed as standard processes. Focus group agendas also can be standard. Standardize as much as possible so that evaluation forms are not reinvented for each application. As a result, tabulation is faster and often less expensive. When this is accomplished, evaluation will be routine.

Use Streamlined Reporting

Reporting data can be one of the most time-consuming parts of evaluation, taking precious time away from collecting, processing, and analyzing data. Yet, reporting is often the most critical part of the process, because many audiences need different information. When the audience understands the evaluation methodology, they can usually digest information in a brief format. For example, it is possible to present the results of a study using a one-page format. It is, however, essential for the audience to understand the approach to evaluation and the principles and assumptions behind the methodology; otherwise, they will not understand what the data mean.

The good news is that many shortcuts can be taken to supply the data necessary for the audience and manage the process in an efficient way. All these shortcuts are important processes that can help make evaluation routine because when evaluation is expensive, time consuming, and difficult, it will never become routine.

Getting It Done

Now it is time to develop your ROI implementation plan using Exercise 7-1. Items may be added or removed so that this becomes a customized document. This plan summarizes key issues presented in the book and will help you as you move beyond the basics of ROI.

Exercise 7-1. Measurement and Evaluation Strategy and Plan

This document addresses a variety of issues that make up the complete measurement and evaluation strategy and plan. Each of the following items should be explored and decisions made regarding the specific approach or issue.

Purposes of Evaluation
From the list of evaluation purposes, select the ones that are relevant to your organization:
- ❑ Determine success in achieving program objectives.
- ❑ Identify strengths and weaknesses in the talent development process.
- ❑ Set priorities for talent development resources.
- ❑ Test the clarity and validity of tests, cases, and exercises.
- ❑ Identify the participants who were most (or least) successful with the program.
- ❑ Reinforce major points made during the program.
- ❑ Decide who should participate in future programs.
- ❑ Compare the benefits to the costs of a talent development program.
- ❑ Enhance the accountability of talent development.
- ❑ Assist in marketing future programs.
- ❑ Determine if a program was an appropriate solution.
- ❑ Establish a database to assist management with decision making.

Are there any others?

Chapter 7

Exercise 7-1. Measurement and Evaluation Strategy and Plan (cont.)

Overall Evaluation Purpose Statement
State the purpose for conducting an evaluation:

Stakeholder Groups
Identify specific stakeholders that are important to the success of measurement and evaluation:

Evaluation Targets and Goals
List the approximate percentage of programs currently evaluated at each level. List the number of programs you plan to evaluate at each level by a specific date.

Level	Current Use	Planned Use	Date
Level 1: Reaction and Planned Action			
Level 2: Learning			
Level 3: Application and Implementation			
Level 4: Impact			
Level 5: ROI			

Staffing
Indicate the philosophy of using internal or external staff for evaluation work and the number of staff involved in this process part time and full time.

- Internal versus external philosophy:

- Number of part-time staff:
  » Names or titles:

- Number of full-time staff:
  » Names or titles:

Responsibilities
Detail the responsibilities of different groups in talent development. Generally, specialists are involved in a leadership role in evaluation, and others are involved in providing support and assistance in different phases of the process.

Group	Responsibilities

Budget

The budget for measurement and evaluation in best-practice organizations is 3 to 5 percent of the learning and development budget. What is your current level of measurement and evaluation investment? What is your target?

Data Collection Methods

Indicate the current data collection methods used and planned for the different levels of evaluation.

	Current Use	Planned Use
Level 1: Reaction and Planned Action		
Questionnaires	❏	❏
Focus groups	❏	❏
Interviews	❏	❏
Level 2: Learning		
Objective tests	❏	❏
Questionnaires and surveys	❏	❏
Simulations	❏	❏
Self-assessments	❏	❏
Level 3: Application and Implementation		
Follow-up surveys	❏	❏
Observations	❏	❏
Interviews	❏	❏
Follow-up focus groups	❏	❏
Action planning	❏	❏
Level 4: Impact		
Follow-up questionnaires	❏	❏
Action planning	❏	❏
Performance contracting	❏	❏
Performance records monitoring	❏	❏

Exercise 7-1. Measurement and Evaluation Strategy and Plan (cont.)

Building Capability
How will staff members develop their measurement and evaluation capability?

Action	Audience	Who Conducts or Organizes?
ROI briefings (one to two hours)		
Half-day ROI workshop		
One-day ROI workshop		
Two-day ROI workshop		
ROI certification		
Coaching		
ROI conferences		
Networking		

Use of Technology
How do you use technology for data collection, integration, and scorecard reporting, including technology for conducting ROI studies? How do you plan to use technology?

Method	Current Use	Planned Use
Surveys	❏	❏
Tests	❏	❏
Other data collection	❏	❏
Integration	❏	❏
ROI	❏	❏
Scorecards	❏	❏

Communication Methods
Indicate the specific methods you currently use to communicate results. What methods do you plan to use?

Method	Current Use	Planned Use
Meetings	❏	❏
Interim and progress reports	❏	❏
Newsletters	❏	❏
Email and electronic media	❏	❏
Brochures and pamphlets	❏	❏
Case studies	❏	❏

Use of Data

Indicate how you currently use evaluation data by placing a "✓" in the appropriate box. Indicate your planned use of evaluation data by placing an "X" in the appropriate box.

Strategy	Appropriate Level of Data				
	1	2	3	4	5
Adjust program design	❏	❏	❏	❏	❏
Improve program delivery	❏	❏	❏	❏	❏
Influence application and impact	❏	❏	❏	❏	❏
Enhance reinforcement for learning	❏	❏	❏	❏	❏
Improve management support for talent development	❏	❏	❏	❏	❏
Improve satisfaction with stakeholders	❏	❏	❏	❏	❏
Recognize and reward participants	❏	❏	❏	❏	❏
Justify or enhance budget	❏	❏	❏	❏	❏
Develop norms and standards	❏	❏	❏	❏	❏
Reduce costs	❏	❏	❏	❏	❏
Market talent development programs	❏	❏	❏	❏	❏
Expand implementation to other areas	❏	❏	❏	❏	❏

Questions or Comments

Appendix
ROI Forecasting Basics

Although beyond the scope of this book, it is important to introduce the basics of forecasting. There are a variety of forecasting techniques available. The most common are of pre-program forecasts, pilot programs, and Level 1 forecasts.

Pre-Program Forecasts

Pre-program forecasts are ideal when you are deciding between two programs designed to solve the same problem. They also serve well when considering one very expensive program or deciding between one or more delivery mechanisms. Whatever your need for pre-program forecasting, the process is similar to post-program ROI evaluation.

When conducting a pre-program forecast, the step of isolating the effects of the program is omitted. It is assumed that the estimated results are referring to the influence on the program under evaluation.

Figure A-1 shows the basic forecast model. An estimate of the change in results data expected to be influenced by the program is the first step in the process. From there data conversion, cost estimates, and the calculation are the same as in post-program analysis. The anticipated intangibles are speculative in forecasting, but they can be indicators of which measures may be influenced beyond those included in the ROI calculation.

Appendix

Figure A-1. Basic ROI Forecasting Model

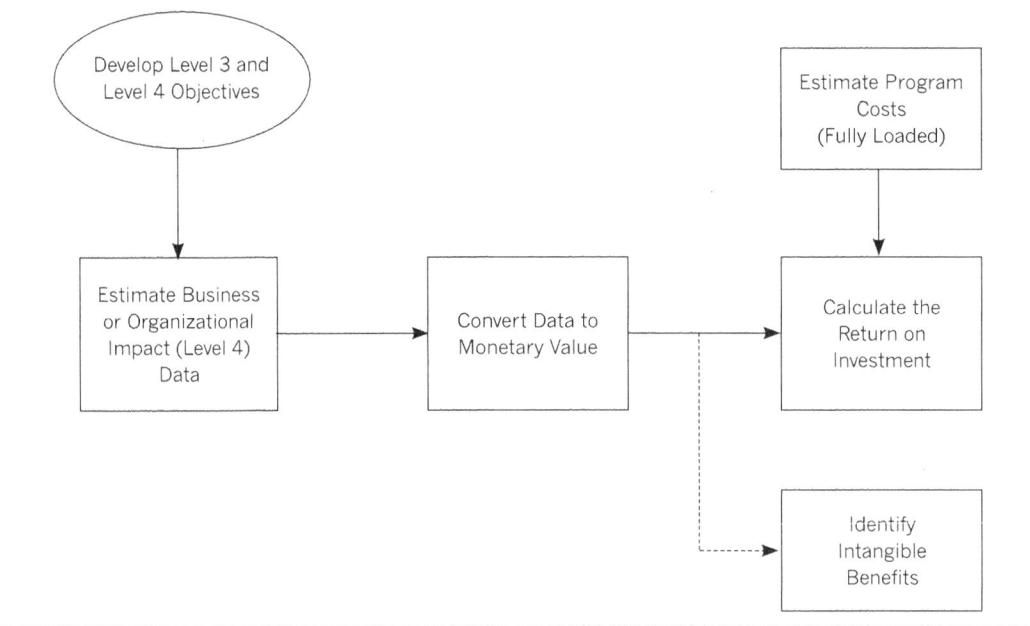

There are 10 steps to develop a pre-program ROI forecast:
1. Develop Levels 3 and 4 objectives with as many specifics as possible.
2. Estimate or forecast the monthly improvement in the business impact data (ΔP).
3. Convert the business impact data to monetary values (V) using one or more of the methods described in chapter 5.
4. Develop the estimated annual impact (ΔI) in monetary terms by multiplying the monthly improvement by the value by 12: $\Delta I = \Delta P \times V \times 12$.
5. Factor additional years into the analysis if a program will have a significant useful life beyond the first year.
6. Estimate the fully loaded cost of the program (C), using the cost summary profile shown in chapter 5.
7. Calculate the forecasted ROI using the total projected benefits and the estimated cost in the standard ROI formula:

$$\text{ROI (\%)} = \frac{\Delta I - C}{C} \times 100$$

8. Use sensitivity analysis to develop several ROI values with different levels of potential improvements.
9. Identify potential intangible benefits by obtaining input from those most knowledgeable of the situation.
10. Communicate the ROI projection and anticipated intangibles with care and caution. Remember: Although you have based the forecast on several clearly defined assumptions, there is still room for error.

Pilot Program

A more accurate forecast of program success is through a small-scale pilot, and then developing ROI based on post-program data. There are five steps to this approach:
1. As in the pre-program forecast, develop Levels 3 and 4 objectives.
2. Initiate the program on a small scale without all the bells and whistles. This keeps the cost low without sacrificing the fundamentals of the program.
3. Fully implement the program with one or more of the typical groups of individuals who can benefit from it.
4. Calculate the ROI using the ROI Methodology for post-program analysis.
5. Decide whether to implement the program throughout the organization based on the results of the pilot program.

Using a pilot post-program evaluation as your ROI forecast will allow you to report the actual story of program success for the pilot group, showing results at all five levels of evaluation, including intangible benefits.

Level 1 Forecasting

A simple approach to forecasting ROI for a new program is to add a few questions to the standard Level 1 evaluation questionnaire. As in the case of pre-program forecast, the data are not as credible as in an actual post-program evaluation; however, a Level 1 evaluation at a minimum relies on data from participants who have actually attended the program.

Table A-1 presents a brief series of questions that can develop a forecast ROI at the end of a program. Using this series of questions, participants detail how they plan to use what they have learned and the results that they expect to achieve. They are asked to convert their anticipated accomplishments into an annual monetary value and show the basis for developing the values; they moderate their response with a confidence estimate to make the data more credible while

Appendix

allowing participants to reflect on their uncertainty with the process. Several adjustments are made to the data to develop the total anticipated monetary benefits. The projected costs are developed to compare with the monetary benefits for an ROI calculation. Though not as reliable as actual data, this process provides some indication of potential program success.

Table A-1. Questions for Forecasting ROI at Level 1

1. As a result of this program, what specific actions will you attempt as you apply what you have learned?
2. Indicate what specific measures, outcomes, or projects will change as a result of your action.
3. As a result of these anticipated changes, estimate (in monetary values) the benefits to your organization over a period of one year. $_____
4. What is the basis of this estimate?
5. What confidence, expressed as a percentage, can you put in your estimate? _____%
   (0% = no confidence; 100% = complete certainty)

Additional Approaches to Forecasting

Other approaches to forecasting include the use of Level 2 test data. A reliable test, reflecting the content of talent development programs, is validated against impact measures. With a statistically significant relationship between test scores and improvement in impact measures, test scores should relate to improved performance. The performance can be converted to monetary value and the test scores can then be used to estimate the monetary impact from the program. When compared to projected costs, the ROI is forecasted.

Another approach is forecasting ROI at Level 3, which places monetary value on competencies. A very basic approach to forecasting ROI using improvement with competencies is to:

1. Identify the competencies.
2. Determine the percentage of the skills applied on the job.
3. Determine the monetary value of the competencies using the salary and benefits of participants.
4. Determine the increase in skill level.
5. Calculate the monetary benefits of the improvement.
6. Compare the monetary benefits to the cost of the program.

Table A-2 presents a basic example of forecasting ROI using Level 3 data.

Table A-2. Example of Forecasting ROI at Level 3

Ten supervisors attend a four-day learning program

1. Identify competencies: Supervisor skills
2. Determine percentage of skills used on the job: 80% (average of group)
3. Determine the monetary value of the competencies using salary and benefits of participants: $40,000 per participant

    Multiply percentage of skills used on the job by the value of the job: $50,000 × 80% = $40,000
    Calculate the dollar value of the competencies for the group: $40,000 × 10 = $400,000

4. Determine increase in skill level: 10% increase (average of group)
5. Calculate the monetary benefits of the improvement: $40,000

    Multiply the dollar value of the competencies by the improvement in skill level: $400,000 × 10% = $40,000

6. Compare the monetary benefits to the cost of the program: The ROI is 166% and the cost of the program is $15,000

$$\text{ROI (\%)} = \frac{\$40,000 - \$15,000}{\$15,000} \times 100 = 166\%$$

A more comprehensive approach to forecasting ROI at Level 3 is the use of utility analysis. Utility analysis should be considered when it is important to provide monetary value to behavior change.

Forecasting is an excellent tool when an actual ROI study is not feasible. A word of caution, however: if you forecast, forecast frequently. It needs to be pursued regularly to build experience and a history of use. Also, it is always helpful to conduct an actual ROI study following a forecast and compare the results to develop better skills for the forecasting process.

Noted

Forecasting ROI and the use of predictive analytics is becoming much more popular than in the past. Be forewarned: Don't rely on forecasting alone. While forecasting and predictive analytics are useful, they result in mere estimates of what could be. The real meaning is in what actually occurs—hence, the need for post-program evaluation.

References

Cascio, W.F. 2000. *Costing Human Resources: The Financial Impact of Behavior in Organizations.* Australia: South-Western College Publishing.

Cross, R., T. Davenport, and P. Gray. 2019. "Demonstrating Impact Through Collaborative Analytics." Connected Commons website.

Delcol, K., S. Wolfe, and K. West, ed. n.d. "Can Innovation Tools Influence the New Product Development Process?" http://debonogroup.com/return-on-investment.htm.

Institute for Corporate Productivity (i4cp) and ROI Institute. 2018. *Four Ways to Advance Your People Analytics Practice.* Seattle, WA: Institute for Corporate Productivity; Birmingham, AL: ROI Institute.

Harris, R.L. 1999. *Information Graphics: A Comprehensive,* Illustrated Reference. New York: Oxford University Press.

Harvard Business Review Analytic Services. 2017. *How CEO's and CHRO's Can Connect People Strategy to Business Strategy.* Boston: Harvard Business Review Publishing.

Heskett, J., W. Sasser, and L. Schlesinger. 1997. *The Service Profit Chain: How Leading Companies Link Profit and Growth to Loyalty, Satisfaction, and Value.* New York: Free Press.

Horngren, C. 1982. *Cost Accounting.* Englewood Cliffs, NJ: Prentice Hall.

Howard, T. 2005. "Brewers Get Into the Spirits of Marketing." *USA Today,* May 16.

Mooij, J.M., J. Peters, D. Janzing, J. Zscheischler, and B. Schölkopf. 2016. "Distinguishing Cause From Effect Using Observational Data: Methods and Benchmarks." *Journal of Machine Learning Research* 17(32): 1–102.

Parker, L., and C. Hubble. 2015. "Measuring ROI in a Supervisory Leadership Development Program." In *Measuring the Success of Leadership Development,* edited by P.P. Phillips, J.J. Phillips, and R.L. Ray. Alexandria, VA: ATD Press.

Phillips, J.J., ed. 1997. *Measuring Return on Investment,* vol. 2. Alexandria, VA: ASTD Press.

Phillips, J.J. 2003. *Return on Investment in Training and Performance Improvement Programs,* 2nd ed. Boston: Butterworth-Heinemann.

Phillips, J.J., and P.P. Phillips. 2005. *ROI at Work.* Alexandria, VA: ASTD Press.

References

Phillips, J.J., and P.P. Phillips. 2009. *Measuring Success: What CEOs Really Thin About Learning Investments.* Alexandria, VA: ASTD Press.

Phillips, J.J., and P.P. Phillips. 2016. *Handbook of Training Evaluation and Measurement,* 4th ed. New York: Routledge.

Phillips, J.J., R.D. Stone, and P.P. Phillips. 2001. *The Human Resources Scorecard: Measuring the Return on Investment.* Boston: Butterworth-Heinemann.

Phillips, P.P., ed. 2001. *Measuring Return on Investment,* vol. 3. Alexandria, VA: ASTD Press.

Phillips, P.P., ed. 2002. *Measuring ROI in the Public Sector.* Alexandria, VA: ASTD Press.

Phillips, P.P. 2017. *The Bottomline on ROI,* 3rd ed. West Chester, PA: HRDQ.

Phillips, P.P., J.J. Phillips, G. Paone, and C. Huff-Gaudet. 2019. *Value for Money: How to Show the Value for Money for All Types of Projects and Programs in Governments, Non-Governmental Organizations, Nonprofits, and Businesses.* Hoboken, NJ: Wiley.

Phillips, P.P., J.J. Phillips, and R.L. Ray. 2016. *Measuring the Success of Employee Engagement: A Step-by-Step Guide for Measuring Impact and Calculating ROI.* Alexandria, VA: ATD Press.

Prest, A.R. 1965. "Cost-Benefit Analysis: A Survey." *The Economic Journal* 75(300): 683–735.

Sibbett, D. 1997. "Harvard Business Review: 75 Years of Management Ideas and Practices 1922–1977." *Harvard Business Review.*

Thompson, M.S. 1980. *Benefit-Cost Analysis for Program Evaluation.* Thousand Oaks, CA: Sage Publications.

Tufte, E.R. 1983. *The Visual Display of Quantitative Information.* Cheshire, CT: Graphics Press.

Wharff, D. 2005. Presentation for ADET E8 Learning Analytics and Strategies: "Serving the Enterprise."

Additional Resources

Following are additional resources available to assist with the understanding, use, and application of the ROI Methodology presented in this book.

Additional Books From the ROI Institute

Elkeles, T., and J.J. Phillips. 2007. *The Chief Learning Officer: Driving Value Within a Changing Organization Through Learning and Development.* Waltham, MA: Butterworth-Heinemann.

Elkeles, T., J.J. Phillips, and P.P. Phillips. 2016. *The Chief Talent Officer: Driving Value Within A Changing Organization Through Learning and Development,* 2nd ed. Abingdon, UK: Routledge.

Phillips, J.J. 2003. *Return on Investment in Training and Performance Improvement Projects,* 2nd ed. New York: Elsevier; Waltham, MA: Butterworth-Heinemann.

Phillips, J.J., W. Brantley, and P.P. Phillips. 2011. *Project Management ROI: A Step-by-Step Guide for Measuring the Impact and ROI for Projects.* Hoboken, NJ: John Wiley.

Phillips, J.J., M.T. Breining, and P.P. Phillips. 2008. *Return on Investment in Meetings & Events: Tools and Techniques to Measure the Success of All Types of Meetings and Events.* Waltham, MA: Butterworth-Heinemann.

Phillips, J.J., V. Buzachero, P.P. Phillips, and Z.L. Phillips. 2012. *Measuring ROI in Healthcare: Tools and Techniques to Measure the Impact and ROI in Healthcare Improvement Projects and Programs.* New York: McGraw-Hill.

Phillips, J.J., M. Myhill, and J.B. McDonough. 2007. *Proving the Value of Meetings & Events: How and Why to Measure ROI.* Birmingham, AL: ROI Institute; Dallas: MPI.

Phillips, J.J., and P.P. Phillips. 2007. *Show Me the Money: How to Determine ROI in People, Projects, and Programs.* San Francisco: Berrett-Koehler.

Phillips, J.J., and P.P. Phillips. 2008. *Beyond Learning Objectives: Develop Powerful Objectives that Link to the Bottom Line.* Alexandria, VA: ASTD Press.

Phillips, J.J., and P.P. Phillips. 2008. *The Measurement and Evaluation Series – ROI Fundamentals 1, Data Collection 2, Isolation of Results 3, Data Conversion 4, Costs and ROI 5, Communication and Implementation 6.* New York: Pfeiffer.

Phillips, J.J., and P.P. Phillips. 2010. *The Consultant's Guide to Results-Driven Proposals. How to Write Proposals That Forecast the Impact and ROI.* New York: McGraw-Hill.

Phillips, J.J., and P.P. Phillips. 2011. *10 Steps to Successful Business Alignment.* Alexandria, VA: ASTD Press.

Phillips, J.J., and P.P. Phillips. 2012. *Proving the Value of HR: How and Why to Measure ROI*. 2nd ed. Alexandria, VA: SHRM.

Phillips, J.J., and P.P. Phillips. 2015. *High-Impact Capital Strategy: Addressing the 12 Major Challenges Today's Organizations Face.* New York: AMACOM.

Phillips, J.J., and P.P. Phillips. 2015. *Making Human Capital Analytics Work: Measuring the ROI of Human Capital Processes and Outcomes.* New York: McGraw-Hill.

Phillips, J.J., and P.P. Phillips. 2016. *Handbook of Training Evaluation and Measurement,* 4th ed. New York: Routledge.

Phillips, J. J., and P.P. Phillips. 2018. *The Value of Innovation: Knowing, Proving, and Showing the Value of Innovation and Creativity.* Hoboken, NJ: Wiley.

Phillips, J.J., P.P. Phillips, and A. Pulliam. 2014. *Measuring ROI in Environment, Health, and Safety.* Hoboken, NJ: Scrivener-Wiley.

Phillips, J.J., P.P. Phillips, and R.L. Ray. 2012. *Measuring Leadership Development: Quantify Your Program's Impact and ROI on Organizational Performance.* New York: McGraw-Hill.

Phillips, J.J., P.P. Phillips, and K. Smith. 2016. *Accountability in Human Resource Management: Connect HR to Business Results,* 2nd ed. Abingdon, UK: Routledge.

Phillips, J.J., and L. Schmidt. 2004. *The Leadership Scorecard* (Improving Human Performance Series). New York: Elsevier; Waltham, MA: Butterworth-Heinemann.

Phillips, J.J., and R. Stone. 2001. *The Human Resources Scorecard: Measuring Return on Investment.* New York: Elsevier; Waltham, MA: Butterworth-Heinemann.

Phillips, J.J., and R. Stone. 2002. *How to Measure Training Results: A Practical Guide to Tracking the Six Key Indicators.* New York: McGraw-Hill.

Phillips, J.J., W.D. Trotter, and P.P. Phillips. 2015. *Maximizing the Value of Consulting: A Guide for Internal and External Consultants.* Hoboken, NJ: Wiley.

Phillips, P.P., ed. 2001. *Measuring Return on Investment* (In Action), vol. 3. Alexandria, VA: ASTD Press.

Phillips, P.P. 2017. *The Bottomline on ROI: Benefits and Barriers to Measuring Learning, Performance Improvement, and Human Resources Programs,* 3rd ed. West Chester, PA: HRDQ.

Phillips, P.P., and J.J. Phillips. 2007. *The Value of Learning: How Organizations Capture Value and ROI and Translate Them into Support, Improvement, and Funds.* New York: Pfeiffer.

Phillips, P.P., and J.J. Phillips. 2011. *The Green Scorecard: Measuring the Return on Investment in Sustainability Initiatives.* Boston: Nicholas Brealey.

Phillips, P.P., and J.J. Phillips. 2013. *Survey Basics: A Complete How-to Guide to Help You: Design Surveys and Questionnaires, Analyze Data and Display Results, and Identify the Best Survey Tool for Your Needs.* Alexandria, VA: ASTD Press.

Phillips, P.P., and J.J. Phillips. 2016. *Real World Evaluation Training: Navigating Common Constraints for Exceptional Results.* Alexandria, VA: ATD Press.

Phillips, P.P., and J.J. Phillips. 2017. *The Business Case for Learning: Using Design Thinking to Deliver Business Results and Increase the Investment in Talent Development.* West Chester, PA: HRDQ; Alexandria, VA: ATD Press

Phillips, P.P., J.J. Phillips, G. Paone, and C. Huff-Gaudet. 2019. *Value for Money: How to Show the Value for Money for All Types of Projects and Programs in Governments, Non-Governmental Organizations, Nonprofits, and Businesses.* Hoboken, NJ: Wiley.

Phillips, P.P., J.J. Phillips, R. Stone, and H. Burkett. 2006. *The ROI Fieldbook: Strategies for Implementing ROI in HR and Training.* Waltham, MA: Butterworth-Heinemann.

Robinson, D.G., J.C. Robinson, J.J. Phillips, P.P. Phillips, and D. Handshaw. 2015. *Performance Consulting: A Strategic Process to Improve, Measure, and Sustain Organizational Results,* 3rd ed. Oakland, CA: Berrett-Koehler.

Case Studies Describing ROI Application

Elkeles, T., P.P. Phillips, and J.J. Phillips. 2014. *Measuring the Success of Learning Through Technology: A Step-by-Step Guide for Measuring Impact and ROI on E-Learning, Blended Learning, and Mobile Learning.* Alexandria, VA: ASTD Press.

Phillips, J.J., ed. 1994. *Measuring Return on Investment* (In Action), vol. 1. Alexandria, VA: ASTD Press.

Phillips, J.J., ed. 1997. *Measuring Return on Investment* (In Action), vol. 2. Alexandria, VA: ASTD Press.

Phillips, J.J., ed. 1998. *Implementing Evaluation Systems and Processes* (In Action). Alexandria, VA: ASTD Press.

Phillips, J.J., ed. 2000. *Performance Analysis and Consulting* (In Action). Alexandria, VA: ASTD Press.

Phillips, J.J., and P.P. Phillips. 2006. *ROI at Work: Best Practice Case Studies From the Real World.* Alexandria, VA: ASTD Press.

Phillips, J.J., and P.P. Phillips. 2010. *Measuring for Success: What CEOs Really Think About Learning Investments.* Birmingham, AL: ROI Institute; Alexandria, VA: ASTD Press.

Phillips, J.J., P.P. Phillips, and L. Zuniga. 2013. *Measuring the Success of Organization Development: A Step-by-Step Guide for Measuring Impact and Calculating ROI.* Alexandria, VA: ASTD Press.

Phillips, J.J., and P.P. Phillips. 2014. *Measuring ROI in Employee Relations and Compliance.* Alexandria, VA: SHRM.

Phillips, P.P., ed. 2001. *Measuring Return on Investment* (In Action), vol. 3. Alexandria, VA: ASTD Press.

Phillips, P.P., and J.J. Phillips. 2002. *Measuring ROI in the Public Sector* (In Action). Alexandria, VA: ASTD Press.

Phillips, P.P., and J.J. Phillips. 2008. *ROI in Action Casebook.* New York: Pfeiffer.

Phillips, P.P., and J.J. Phillips. 2012. *Measuring the Success of Coaching: A Step-by-Step Guide for Measuring Impact and Calculating ROI.* Alexandria, VA: ASTD Press.

Phillips, P.P., and J.J. Phillips. 2012. *Measuring ROI in Learning and Development: Case Studies from Global Organizations.* Alexandria, VA: ASTD Press.

Phillips, P.P., and J.J. Phillips. 2013. *Measuring the Success of Sales Training: A Step-by-Step Guide for Measuring Impact and Calculating ROI.* Alexandria, VA: ASTD Press.

Phillips, P.P., J.J. Phillips, and R.L. Ray. 2015. *Measuring the Success of Leadership Development: A Step-by-Step Guide for Measuring Impact and Calculating ROI.* Alexandria, VA: ATD.

Phillips, P.P., and J.J. Phillips. 2016. *Measuring the Success of Employee Engagement: A Step-by-Step Guide for Measuring Impact and Calculating ROI.* Alexandria, VA: ATD Press.

Phillips, P.P., and J.J. Phillips. 2018. *Value for Money: Measuring the Return on Non-Capital Investments.* Birmingham, AL: BWE Press.

Pope, C., and J.J. Phillips, eds. 2001. *Implementing E-learning Solutions* (In Action). Alexandria, VA: ASTD Press.

Schmidt, L., and J.J. Phillips, eds. 2003. *Implementing Training Scorecards* (In Action). Alexandria, VA: ASTD Press.

TD at Work (formerly Infoline): The How-to Reference Tool for Training and Performance Professionals

The *TD at Work* series from ATD offers tools, templates, and job aids on a variety of topics. The following focus on each of the five levels of evaluation discussed in this book:

American Society for Training & Development (ASTD). 2009. "The Four Levels of Evaluation + ROI." *Infoline.* Alexandria, VA: ASTD Press.

Anand, P. 2017. "Executive Dashboards to Win Over the C-Suite." *TD at Work.* Alexandria, VA: ATD Press.

Association for Talent Development (ATD). 2015. "Train the Trainer Volume 4: Measurement and Evaluation: Essentials for Measuring Training Success." *TD at Work.* Alexandria, VA: ATD Press.

Burkett, H. 2013. "10 Tactics for a Sustainable Evaluation Process." *Infoline.* Alexandria, VA: ASTD Press.

Burkett, H., and P.P. Phillips. 2001. "Managing Evaluation Shortcuts." *Infoline.* Alexandria, VA: ASTD Press.

DeTuncq, T. 2012. "Demystifying Measurement & Evaluation." *Infoline.* Alexandria, VA: ASTD Press.

Downs, L. 2015. "Managing Learning Programs." *TD at Work.* Alexandria, VA: ATD Press.

Glynn, K., and D. Tolsma. 2017. "Design Thinking Meets ADDIE." *TD at Work.* Alexandria, VA: ATD Press.

Guerra-López, L., and K. Hicks. 2015. "Turning Trainers into Strategic Business Partners." *TD at Work.* Alexandria, VA: ATD Press.

Levenson, A. 2016. "Measuring and Maximizing the Impact of Talent Development." *TD at Work.* Alexandria, VA: ATD Press.

Neal, B. 2014. "How to Develop Training Quality Standards." *Infoline.* Alexandria, VA: ASTD Press.

Novak, C. 2012. "Making the Financial Case for Performance Improvement." *Infoline.* Alexandria, VA: ASTD Press.

Phillips, J.J., W. Jones, and C. Schmidt. 1999. "Level 3 Evaluation: Application." *Infoline.* Alexandria, VA: ASTD Press.

Phillips, J.J., and P.P. Phillips. 1998. "Level 5 Evaluation: Mastering ROI." *Infoline.* Alexandria, VA: ASTD Press.

Phillips, J.J., R.. Shriver, and H.S. Giles. 1999. "Level 2 Evaluation: Learning." *Infoline.* Alexandria, VA: ASTD Press.

Phillips, J.J., and R.D. Stone. 1999. "Level 4 Evaluation: Business Results." *Infoline.* Alexandria, VA: ASTD Press.

Phillips, J.J., J.O. Wright, and S.I. Pettit-Sleet. 1999. "Level 1 Evaluation: Reaction and Planned Action." *Infoline.* Alexandria, VA: ASTD Press.

Phillips, P.P., and J.J. Phillips. 2003. "Evaluation Data: Planning and Use." *Infoline.* Alexandria, VA: ASTD Press.

Spitzer, D., and M. Conway. 2002. "Link Training to the Bottom Line." *Infoline.* Alexandria, VA: ASTD Press.

Waagen, A. 1997. "Essentials for Evaluation." *Infoline.* Alexandria, VA: ASTD Press.

Books on Data Visualization

Few, S. 2012. *Show Me the Numbers: Designing Tables and Graphs to Enlighten,* 2nd ed. Burlingame, CA: Analytics Press.

Knaflic, C.N. 2015. *Storytelling With Data: A Data Visualization Guide for Business Professionals.* Hoboken, NJ: Wiley Publishing.

Tufte, E.R. 1990. *Envisioning Information.* Cheshire, CT: Graphics Press.

Tufte, E.R. 1997. *Visual Explanations: Images and Quantities, Evidence and Narrative.* Cheshire, CT: Graphics Press.

Wilke, C.O. 2019. *Fundamentals of Data Visualization: A Primer on Making Informative and Compelling Figures.* Sebastopol, CA: O'Reilly Media.

About the Authors

Patricia P. Phillips, PhD, is CEO of ROI Institute Inc. the leading source of ROI competency building, implementation support, networking, and research. A renowned leader in measurement and evaluation, she helps organizations implement the ROI Methodology in 70 countries. Patti serves as a member of the Board of Trustees of the United Nations Institute for Training and Research (UNITAR). In addition, she serves as chair of the Institute for Corporate Productivity (i4cp) People Analytics Board; principal research fellow for The Conference Board; board member of the Center for Talent Reporting; and ATD CPLP Certification Institute fellow. Patti also serves on the faculty of the UN System Staff College in Turin, Italy. Her work has been featured on CNBC, EuroNews, and more than a dozen business journals.

Patti's academic accomplishments include a PhD in international development and a master's degree in public and private management. She is a certified in ROI evaluation and has been awarded the designations of Certified Professional in Learning and Performance and Certified Performance Technologist.

Patti, along with her husband, Jack J. Phillips, contributes to a variety of journals and has authored a number of books on the subject of measurement, evaluation, analytics, and ROI. She can be reached at patti@roiinstitute.net.

Jack J. Phillips, PhD, is a world-renowned expert on accountability, measurement, and evaluation. He provides consulting services for Fortune 500 companies and major global organizations. The author or editor of more than 100 books, he conducts workshops and presents at conferences throughout the world.

Jack has received several awards for his books and work. On three occasions, *Meeting News* named him one of the 25 Most Powerful People in the Meetings and Events

Industry, based on his work on ROI. The Society for Human Resource Management presented him an award for one of his books and honored a Phillips ROI study with its highest award for creativity. The Association for Talent Development, formerly the American Society of Training & Development, gave him its highest award, Distinguished Contribution to Workplace Learning and Development for his work on ROI. The International Society for Performance Improvement presented Jack with its highest award, the Thomas F. Gilbert Award, for his contribution to human performance technology. His work has been featured in the *Wall Street Journal, Business-Week,* and *Fortune* magazine. He has been interviewed by several television programs, including CNN. He served as president of the International Society for Performance Improvement.

Jack regularly consults with clients in manufacturing, service, and government organizations in 70 countries. He and his wife, Patti P. Phillips, contribute to a variety of journals in addition to authoring more than 100 books.

Jack has undergraduate degrees in electrical engineering, physics, and mathematics; a master's degree in decision sciences from Georgia State University; and a PhD in human resource management from the University of Alabama. He has served on the boards of several private businesses—including two NASDAQ companies—and several nonprofits and associations, including the Association for Talent Development and the National Management Association. He is chairman of ROI Institute Inc. and can be reached at jack@roiinstitute.net.

About ROI Institute

ROI Institute Inc. is the leading resource on research, training, and networking for practitioners of the ROI Methodology. Founders and owners Patti P. Phillips, PhD, and Jack J. Phillips, PhD, are the leading experts in the application of ROI to learning, HR, and performance improvement programs.

Founded in 1993, ROI Institute is a service-driven organization assisting professionals in improving their programs and processes through the use of the ROI Methodology. This methodology is a critical tool for measuring and evaluating programs with more than 26 different applications in more than 70 countries.

ROI Institute offers a variety of consulting services, learning opportunities, and publications. In addition, it conducts research activities for organizations internally, as well as for other enterprises, public sector entities, industries, and interest groups, globally. ROI Institute is the only organization offering ROI Certification to build expertise in implementing ROI evaluation and sustaining the measurement and evaluation process in your organization.

For more information on certification, workshops, consulting and research, visit www.roiinstitute.net, email info@roiinstitute.net, or call 205.678.8101.